JOE MAUER

From Hometown Hero to MVP

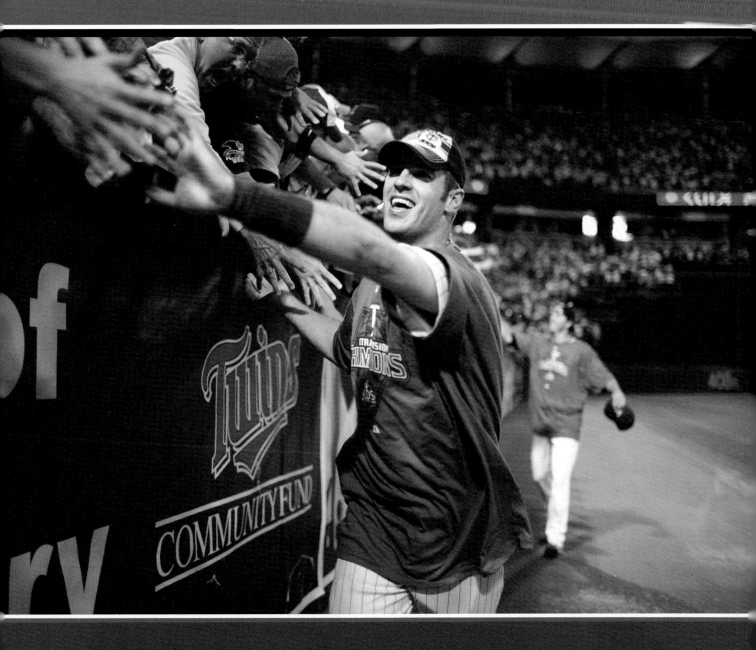

TRIUMPH BOOKS

StarTribune

This book is available in quantity at special discounts for your group or organization. For further information, contact:

Triumph Books
542 South Dearborn Street
Suite 750
Chicago, Illinois 60605
(312) 939-3330
Fax (312) 663-3557
www.triumphbooks.com

Printed in U.S.A.
ISBN: 978-1-60078-503-0

Cover design by Paul Petrowsky
Page design and packaging by Mojo Media, Inc.: Joe Funk and Jason Hinman

Star Tribune
Publisher & CEO: Mike Klingensmith

Editorial Team
Editor, Senior Vice President: Nancy Barnes
Assistant Managing Editor, Sports: Glen Crevier
Senior Photo Editor: Deb Pastner
Sports Photo Director: Tom Sweeney
Reporters: Roman Augustoviz, Joe Christensen, Chip Scoggins, John Millea, La Velle E. Neal III
Columnists: Patrick Reusse, Jim Souhan
Photographers: Bruce Bisping, David Brewster, Elizabeth Flores, Jim Gehrz, Carlos Gonzalez, Kyndell Harkness, Jerry Holt, David Joles, Renee Jones Schneider, Marlin Levison, Brian Peterson, Richard Sennott, Richard Tsong-Taatarii, Jeff Wheeler

Business Team
Senior Vice President, Advertising: David Walsh
Vice President, Classified Advertising/Niche Products: Jamie Flaws
Director of Niche Products: Christina Savin
Project Manager: Lori Sebastian

Website: www.StarTribune.com

The feature stories in this book were previously published in the *Star Tribune* and are all copyright © 2001–2009 Star Tribune Media Company LLC.

contents

Foreword

Arvesta Kelly Sr. took a photo of St. Paul's Jimmy Lee Playground team when the youngsters played in the Timberwolves/Target basketball tournament in 1992.

Nine-year-old Joe Mauer isn't tough to find in the photo. He's the only white kid.

Even back then, all Mauer was interested in was where he could find the best athletic competition. Griggs was the playground closest to the Mauer home, but Jimmy Lee housed the best organization, the best basketball players, and the best pickup games in the summer, so that's where young Joe headed to play his hoops.

Jake Jr., Joe's oldest brother, said: "He spent hours at [Jimmy Lee] playing basketball with kids like Mo Hargrow, who played for the Gophers.

"Joe was the Gatorade National Player of the Year in football and the No. 1 pick in the baseball draft as a high school senior. What people don't realize is that basketball probably was his favorite sport as a kid."

Mauer was a 6-foot-3 point guard and excellent shooter for a Cretin–Derham Hall team that lost in the Minnesota state semis when Joe was a senior. He was the quarterback on a football team that won the state championship when he was a junior in 1999, and lost in the finals in his senior year.

He signed with Florida State on February 1, 2001—two months after Chris Weinke, another Cretin–Derham

Hall quarterback, had won the Heisman Trophy for the same school. Weinke was 28 when he received the award, having enrolled at Florida State after a failed baseball career. Weinke couldn't hit enough to rise through the minors. That wasn't a problem that Mauer figured to face.

Mauer was Cretin–Derham Hall's catcher for three years. He had 222 at-bats in those three high school seasons, striking out once–ONCE–and batting .567.

The Twins had the first selection in the 2001 June draft, based on their latest horrendous season in a streak of eight consecutive losing seasons. This was a draft in which college stars Mark Prior and Mark Teixeira were available. They also were demanding huge dollars to sign.

When the Twins took Mauer, there was an accusation that it a money-saving move. Terry Ryan, the general manager, said there was one reason Mauer was selected: He was the player with the highest potential.

Mauer was the Twins' starting catcher on Opening Day 2004, after only three minor league seasons. Now, six seasons later, he is an American League MVP, having earned it in 2009 while also winning a third batting title.

That's the fact that has to blow any baseball person's mind: From 1901 through 2005, a catcher never won an AL batting title. And now the left-handed-hit-

ting Mauer has won three in the past four years—and he turned 27 on April 19.

Mauer guards his swings zealously. His patience goes beyond getting into hitter's counts. Even if he's down 0-1 or even at 1-1, Mauer is willing to take a second strike if he sees it as a pitcher's pitch—meaning, a pitch that makes him the underdog as a hitter.

Jake Mauer, his dad, has a succinct explanation for his youngest son's remarkable talent: "Joe could hit when he was in diapers." And there's a family photo to prove it—toddler Joe taking what appears to be a level swing with diapers visible under his short pants.

Paul Molitor, another Cretin graduate and a Hall of Famer, wraps up the Mauer effect on his home state thusly: "He's on his way to becoming the most popular athlete in Minnesota history."

—Patrick Reusse

Joseph Patrick Mauer pictured with the Jimmy Lee Playground basketball team in 1992.

The Minnesota Profile

An exclusive look at the Joe Mauer you don't know

Jim Souhan • July 12, 2009

It is early in the day, and Joe Mauer is on his way to the ballpark. He makes one stop on this sunny Friday morning, ducking his 6-5 frame through the door of Schmidty's Sports Barbers. Dressed casually in a T-shirt, jeans, and Nikes, he settles into the chair near the window, beneath a framed version of his Twins jersey. The proprietor, John Schmidt, wraps a cloth around his neck and administers to Minnesota's most famous sideburns as they chat quietly of old friends.

In another city or setting, the brown hair drifting to the floor like confetti might wind up on eBay, but this is St. Paul, and the baseball field visible through the window is the Cretin High diamond where big-league scouts first spotted the owner of those sideburns, and the kid in the barber chair is a Schmidty's regular because of the price of fame, not because of the $17 haircut.

This summer, Mauer has transcended his already-sublime career arc to become one of the best and most popular players in baseball. After a back problem ruined his spring, he returned from the disabled list in early May and started swinging like a latter-day Ted Williams, flirting with .400 and displaying newfound power while eliciting ovations in Chicago's Wrigley Field and Milwaukee's Miller Park, as well as the usual marriage proposals at the Metrodome.

"He's on his way," said fellow Cretin alum, former Twin and baseball Hall of Famer Paul Molitor, "to becoming the most popular athlete in Minnesota history."

Mauer, 26, is the rare big-league superstar who started his career and achieved national stardom with his hometown team, creating a lifestyle as tart as it is sweet. Schmidty's is one of the few places in St. Paul where he can taste normalcy, where his sideburns are trimmed, not adored.

"We've had discussions about how he can come in here and be normal, and everything's like it should be," said Schmidt, who coached Mauer at Cretin–Derham Hall before taking over the barbershop. "I gave him a haircut right before he went over to TwinsFest this winter, and I said, 'You can sit here and everything's cool, and in a few hours you're going to go over there and it's going to be like 'Aaaaaaah!' That's got to blow your mind. It's like two worlds in the same city.

"Joe said, 'Yeah, it's different.'"

One time a kid spotted him at Schmidty's and started a cell phone tree, gathering all of his buddies outside the door, and Mauer shook their hands and took pictures with them, but most days he prefers the illusion of anonymity.

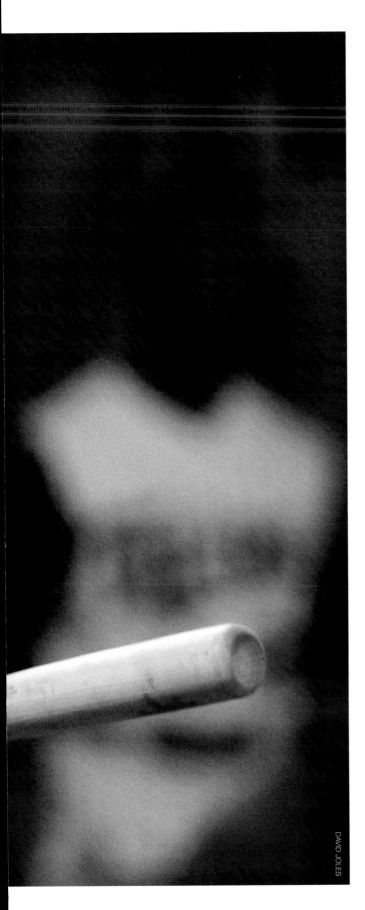

DAVID JOLES

"Being able to do the things I've been able to do, sometimes people do treat you different," Mauer said. "I really appreciate the guys at the barbershop, and all my old friends, because they always treat me the same."

He shrugs, smiles. "The guys in the barbershop just know I'm not that cool."

IT IS EARLY IN THE DAY, and Joe Mauer is on his way to the ballpark. On this sunny Saturday, he is heading from his St. Paul condo to the Metrodome just as two of his best friends, Tony Leseman and Kevin Salmen, settle into a booth at one of their favorite St. Paul joints.

Just about every patron at Shamrock's drops by to talk to Leseman and Salmen. Filled with sports fans, this is exactly the kind of setting that makes Mauer wary.

Salmen played football with Mauer at Cretin, then at the University of Minnesota. Leseman played baseball with Mauer at Cretin, and now lives with him. When Mauer began riding minor league buses between Elizabethton and Johnson City, Tennessee, Leseman and Salmen were enjoying college life. "After he made it to the bigs, everything changed," Leseman said. "I'm on campus, hanging out, and I see these girls, cute girls, wearing Twins jerseys. They walk by, and I'm like, 'Mauer? Hey—what are you doing wearing my buddy's jersey?' That didn't seem quite right."

Mauer is Minnesota's most eligible bachelor, and one of its most reluctant. He's single, friendly, worth millions, and wary of any entanglement that might distract from his career or nudge aside his lifelong friends. His one publicized relationship, with former Miss USA Chelsea Cooley, "kind of bugged him, that so much was made of it," said his best baseball friend, Twins slugger Justin Morneau.

His family and friends didn't mind.

"We kind of liked hanging out with Miss USA," said his father, Jake.

"Where do you go from Miss USA?" Leseman said.

"He's gotta go for Miss World," Salmen said.

"She was a real nice girl," Mauer said. "I think we were at different places in our lives."

When Morneau won the American League Most Valuable Player Award in 2006, a few teammates credited Mauer with helping Morneau learn to stay in. Morneau says he taught Mauer how to go out.

"Let's just say we were good for each other," Morneau said. "I love it when I can get him to go out, because then everyone leaves me alone. He's such a nice guy, he never says no, so everybody can come up to him and he'll have a conversation. And around here, it's not just a conversation. Everyone has a connection. Everyone has a cousin who went to school with him or an uncle who played ball with his father."

Watching him navigate life as a star is like watching Jimmy Stewart star in *Transformers*. "Joe Mauer is *Shaft*, 2009," Salmen said. "The ladies all want to be with him, and the men all want to be him."

IT IS EARLY IN THE DAY, and Joe Mauer is at the ballpark. For someone who spends most of his time around the clubhouse, he's rarely visible. His locker in the Metrodome is in the back right corner, leaving him one step to the training room.

Morneau says Mauer sleeps up to 12 hours a night, sometimes waking just in time to drive to the Metrodome to begin a routine that will last 10 or 11 hours, flanking the game with weightlifting, stretching, hydrotherapy, ice treatments, film study, and game planning meetings.

Reporters are allowed in big-league clubhouses 3½ hours before the game, and must leave an hour before the first pitch. During access time, Mauer will step quickly out of the back rooms to change the music on the sound system, or to retrieve something from his locker, but he doesn't stand still long, knowing that any sign of stillness will lead to interview requests. As his average hovered around .400 this summer, those requests increasingly came from people he didn't know.

At the end of a recent homestand, Mauer emerged from the trainer's room to a waiting group of reporters, managed a smile and said, "What's up, guys?" After a group interview, he turned and told someone, "I need to get on the road."

While Mauer has wearied of talking about himself, his teammates and family members treat him like the little brother he was in the Mauer house on Lexington, the little brother you tease because you can't beat him.

"Did you know he raps?" asked outfielder Michael Cuddyer. "Records his own songs. They're on his iPod."

"You should see him snap," said catcher Mike Redmond. "Everyone thinks he's always even-keeled, but I've always told him as he gets older he's going to get saltier. I'll hear him go in the room behind the dugout and smash a helmet, and I'll pump my fist and say, 'Yes!'"

"He probably won't want this out there, but he is a great dancer," said older brother Jake, and, indeed, Joe admits to mastering the moves to Michael Jackson's "Thriller" when he was young.

"He actually trash-talks me," Morneau said. "We'll be playing basketball, and he just knows he can beat you, and he can't help it."

IT IS LATE IN THE DAY, and Joe Mauer is leaving the ballpark. It is a Sunday night before a rare day off in

the Twins' June schedule, and Mauer is driving an hour north to his cabin.

"I wanted this to be a special place where I could get away, and my whole family could enjoy themselves," Mauer said. "I wanted it to be something that would stay in the family forever."

Mauer's friends call it "the ranch," and say it's more mansion on the hill than little house on the prairie. Mauer spends as much time as he can there during the summer, with family and old friends.

"That place," said childhood friend Hart Smith, "is man-tastic."

The ranch features a movie theater, bowling alley, batting cage, hydrotherapy pool with underwater treadmill, an oxygen room, flat-screen TVs, a recording booth for his budding rap career, swaths of land for hunting and hiking, and a pond good for fishing or hockey.

"I'm so proud of him, because he hasn't spent his money extravagantly on anything selfish," said his father, who is known as Big Jake to distinguish him from Grandpa Jake and Little Jake. "The only thing he's really spent much money on is the ranch."

Smith says the ranch might as well be a kids' clubhouse in the woods with a "No Girls 'Lowed" sign on the door.

"His brothers and friends bring wives up there," Smith said. "For Joe, it's just a place he can be himself."

Which is a pretty good someone to be these days. He's the only American League catcher to win a batting title, and he's done it twice. He owns one Gold Glove, two Silver Sluggers (awarded to the best hitter at each position in the league) and was just named to his third All-Star team. Despite missing a month because of injury, he finished second in the American League in All-Star votes.

Mauer honed his silky, inside-out swing in the

The Mauer File

• Born April, 19, 1983, the youngest of Jake and Teresa Mauer's three children. His brothers, Jake and Bill, played in the Twins' minor-league system, and Jake is the manager of the Gulf Coast (rookie) League Twins.

• Grew up on Lexington Avenue in St. Paul, where, when it was too cold to play sports outside, he would take swings in the garage or make up baseball-related games to play in the basement with his brothers.

• Lives in a condo in St. Paul and owns a ranch an hour north of the Twin Cities, as well as a place in Fort Myers, Florida, where he spends much of the winter.

• Struck out only once during his high school career at Cretin–Derham Hall.

• Became the national high school football player of the year as a Cretin quarterback, and starred on the basketball team.

• No nickname for him has ever stuck, although former teammate Jacques Jones combined a couple in calling him "Super Joe the Natural."

• Became the first pick in the talent-rich 2001 draft when his hometown Twins chose him over renowned college pitcher Mark Prior. Prior is no longer in the majors.

• Has a Lab puppy he named Lil' Kim. (He likes rap, R&B, and hip-hop.)

• The song that plays when he comes to the plate at the Metrodome is TI's "What You Know." He won his first of two batting titles—the only two ever won by an American League catcher—hitting to that song in 2006, and now "My teammates won't let me change it," Mauer said.

• What he sees when he's hitting well: "Everything slows down. It feels like you can almost place the ball wherever you want to."

garage and basement of the Mauer home, often using a device his father invented—a series of pipes that drop a ball into the hitting zone, encouraging an efficient stroke. When Mauer's fame grew, that device became the Mauer QuickSwing.

"He wouldn't hesitate to come home from a football practice and go out to the garage and take 50 swings," Big Jake said.

Teresa said, "Then his brother Jake would finish his homework and go down there and say, 'I bet I can hit nine out of 10,' and they'd challenge each other."

"I was day care for those boys," Grandpa Jake said. "For nine years, every day in the back yard, I took those kids, and we played ball. I made him hit left-handed. We used to tie ropes on their heels and ankles so they wouldn't overstride. When Joe was little, he wanted to swing like Kirby Puckett, but I taught him to keep that foot down, and now look at him."

Smith said: "When Jake and I were 11 and Crazy Billy was 9 and Joe was 7, we'd go down to Griggs playground and play home-run derby. The first summer, the older kids would kick butt, and we'd make Joe have to go get all the balls. The next year, Joe was 8, and he started to win.

"That's the way it's always been, though. I played hockey as a kid; the Mauers played basketball. So now Joe builds the cabin, and we go up there and play hockey, and all of a sudden Joe, who I didn't think even knew how to skate, is the best player on the ice. Which, again, is very annoying.

"Where you can get some guys mad, get them off their game that way, you get Joe mad and he'll just beat you worse, then skate by and tap you on the butt, like, 'You have no chance.'"

Joe Mauer received his monthly haircut from friend and former coach John Schmidty at Schmidty's Sports Barbers. Mauer has known Schmidty since he was a freshman in high school, which is just kitty-corner to the barber shop.

ELIZABETH FLORES

Mauer dominates in Ping Pong (left- and right-handed), bowling (left- and righthanded), golf, basketball (he was a standout in high school), football (he was the national player of the year and a Florida State recruit as a senior), and hockey.

"He's even good," said Salmen, "at splitting wood."

His only flaws as a baseball player before this season were his lack of durability and lack of home-run power, and he seems intent on eradicating both. Playing the most demanding position in the game, he has played in 63 of 66 games since coming off the disabled list and yet is hitting .381 with 15 home runs in 236 at-bats.

This is the guy who, in a recent conversation about golf, said, "I wish I could be good."

IT IS EARLY IN THE DAY, and Joe Mauer is at the ballpark. He's stretching in the back room when his buddy Morneau emerges and tells you more about Mauer than he would ever reveal about himself.

Morneau says Mauer has two goals. "He wants to win the World Series," Morneau said. "And he wants to become one of the best to ever play the game."

That first desire could alter Mauer's sweet, hometown story. His friends and family members say he never talks about money, only about the opportunity to win. His current contract expires after the 2010 season, the Twins' first in new Target Field.

Morneau said Mauer's decision whether to re-sign with the Twins will be affected by the front office's aggressiveness, either during the offseason or at the trading deadline.

"We've been so close at the deadline so many times," Morneau said. "If he feels like we're content being that team that is just good enough not to lose, but everybody is going to have to have a career year for us to scrape into the playoffs, I think that's going to affect his decision a lot.

"It's frustrating going out every day and hearing that 'We want to win a World Series,' and then not seeing more aggressiveness. I think something like that is going to affect his decision more than the value of the contract. We've already got all the money we're ever going to need."

"Isn't that why you play?" Mauer said. "To win championships? If I hit .250 and we won the World Series, I'd be happier than anyone."

IT IS EARLY IN THE DAY, and Joe Mauer is at the ballpark. It is a blistering Tuesday afternoon in Milwaukee, and as he takes extra swings in an anteroom by the visiting clubhouse in Miller Park, his parents tailgate amid thousands of Brewers fans in the parking lot.

Big Jake looks at the sun, inhales the smell of roasting bratwurst and says, "Isn't this what baseball is all about?"

His mother says that Joe's famous calm is often a facade. "He's got a long fuse," Teresa said, "but you don't want to see it run out."

When he was in middle school, Mauer often wrestled with his brothers. One afternoon, Bill angered Joe and Joe flashed what his brothers call "the look." Bill sprinted upstairs to the only room in the house with a lock—a bathroom with a stained glass window on the door. He slammed and locked the door, then exhaled.

Joe smashed his hands through the window and grabbed Bill.

"I remember one time," Teresa said, "when Joe was 5 or 6, and Billy made him mad, and I had hold of Joe, with both arms around him, and he was just focused in on Billy, like a laser. He was growling."

"Of the three," said the boys' grandfather, "Joe was the mean one. The other boys wanted no part of him."

IT IS EARLY IN THE DAY, and Joe Mauer is at the ballpark. He has left the visitor's air-conditioned clubhouse at Miller Park to chat in the dugout before the game. The dugout feels like a convection oven. Mauer is not sweating. He does just about everything calmly, coolly. Walks. Talks. Dresses. Considers. The only time he seems to be in a hurry is when the public closes in. He sprints in and out of the Twins' dugout, at home and on the road, so he won't have to explain to screaming fans why he can't sign 3,000 autographs.

Morneau worries that Mauer's popularity in his hometown will chase him to a larger market, where he might become more anonymous away from the ballpark. Playing in his hometown, Mauer says, is all he's ever known. "I was drafted by the Twins. This is all I have to go on, about being a big-league baseball player, is playing at home. It gets a little crazy at times, but I've tried to manage it as best I can. This is my sixth season, and I know what to expect, at least."

Mauer is a modern-day Peter Pan, still the nice kid from down the street who plays ball every day, even as his friends move on.

Morneau lived with Mauer until Morneau got married. Leseman moved in, and now he's getting married and moving out, and will be replaced as Mauer's roommate by another old buddy, Larry Nava.

"It's nice to have a friend living there, someone who can take care of the place when we go on a 10-day road trip," Mauer said. "These guys are my best friends, and I trust them more than anybody. They're like my brothers."

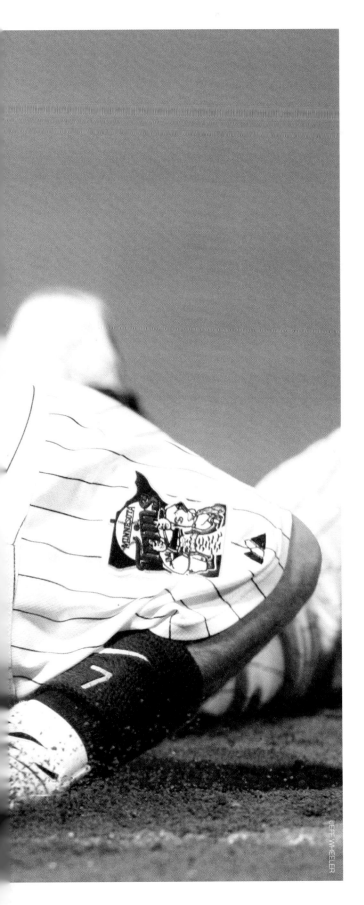

His friends say that Mauer has found a few places he can eat without causing a riot. "If I keep to the same spots, it's fine," he said. "Most of the people that come up are just genuine fans, and that's always nice to see. Just going grocery shopping, though, that can turn a 20-minute trip into a 45-minute or an hour conversation. It's little things like that. All the encounters I've had have been positive, though. I think it's pretty neat."

When he does date these days, he usually relies on his friends to set him up. He wound up with Miss USA because of an old minor league teammate. "It's tough to meet people for the right reasons," he said. "But I'm still young, and I'm having fun. It will happen when it happens. I can imagine settling down. It would have to be the right person, though. I'm not a guy who's an all-night partier. I like to go out and have a good time once in a while, but I'm more of a homebody. I'm a little more low-key than most guys who are in the big leagues."

IT IS EARLY IN THE DAY, and Mauer is about to leave for the ballpark. He is sitting in the corner chair at Schmidty's, glancing at the Cretin baseball diamond he and Paul Molitor made famous among generations of baseball scouts.

"If you want to build your organization around a player who provides leadership, stability and represents your club in the highest possible fashion on and off the field, I don't know how many guys out there can match Joe," Molitor said. "To have all of that, and have that guy be playing in his hometown, while your franchise is preparing to go into a new ballpark, and he's your cornerstone player? That is an amazing and rare thing."

Above Mauer's freshly trimmed head is his jersey, and an old *Sports Illustrated* cover he signed: "To Schmidty's: Thanks for making me look good."

These days, Schmidty's might have the easiest job in America. ●

Sportsperson of the Year

His family's competitiveness and genes produced a phenom in Joe Mauer

Jim Souhan • December 25, 2001

The sky over the Twins' minor league complex is the usual azure. In the shade of the batting cages on this December morning, Jake Mauer pitches scuffed baseballs to Joe Mauer. Their conversation could fill half a postcard.

"Last one," Jake says, quietly, before insisting on "one more" when unsatisfied with his brother's last swing.

Two of the three brothers Mauer have spent much of the fall and winter in Fort Myers. Joe bought a house here with part of his $5 million signing bonus as the Twins' first draft pick, and the brothers played in the instructional league here before beginning their winter workouts.

Joe's exploits in three sports at Cretin–Derham Hall High School have made him the *Star Tribune's* Sportsperson of the Year for 2001. But it is Jake, a second-team All-America from St. Thomas taken by the Twins in the 23rd round, who presides over these daily sessions like a surrogate father figure—prodding Joe, probing his weaknesses, pushing his body.

For while all of the St. Paul Mauers love baseball, it is Joe whom the game loves back. One of Joe's earliest memories is of having a bat handed to him in his crib. "He had a nice swing when he was in diapers," said his father, Jake Jr.

There is proof of this outrageous claim. When Joe was 3 or 4, his grandfather took the three Mauer boys—Jake III, Bill, and Joe—to the grand opening of the Grand Slam batting cages. Channel 9 covered the event but missed the real story.

The Mauers still have the videotape of little Joe, diapers hanging out of his shorts, unleashing a swing that is the graceful product of optimal genetics, environment, and instruction.

Jake Jr. can't count all the baseball players in his extended family. His father and three uncles all played professionally, while Jake himself chose to become a baseball coach after playing at St. Agnes High. It was while coaching that he met his wife, Teresa. The circumstances: Her softball teammates dragged her to a ballfield to meet this cute guy named Jake.

"It figures that we met near a baseball diamond," Teresa said.

Joe never had to leave the house to find quality instruction and competition. Jake III and Bill, now a pitcher at Concordia–St. Paul, would make Joe the runner in games of "Hot Box" in the basement. Jake and Bill would man imaginary bases, and Joe would sprint between them, trying to slide in safely.

"I remember going downstairs one day to do some

Studio portrait of Joe Mauer, all-world quarterback at Cretin–Derham High School, when he was being projected as the possible first-round draft pick in Major League Baseball.

MAX BECHERER

laundry, and seeing Joe sliding headfirst on the concrete floor," Teresa said. "I was about to say something, then I thought, 'What good will it do?' That might have been the first sign we saw that Joe was going to be that competitive. That was also one of the reasons we never finished the basement."

Teresa said Joe has a "long fuse" but a powerful temper once ignited. One of the family's favorite stories is of the time Bill and Joe were wrestling, and Bill suffered the misfortune of getting a good shot in.

Joe chased him up the stairs; Bill locked himself in the bathroom. Then, in a scene out of a bad horror movie, Joe's hand burst through the smoked-glass window and grabbed Bill around the throat.

"Then I realized what I had done," Joe said. He put a gash in his forearm, costing him two weeks of football practice. "The coach was very angry," Teresa said. "He got all over Bill."

Bill? "Yeah, well, he was the one who should have

known better," Teresa said.

The boys usually channeled their energy toward more productive exertions. Jake Jr. installed a home-made hitting machine, in which a ball drops from a tube into the strike zone, teaching a compact stroke and quick hands.

"We're going to start marketing it," Jake Jr. said. "It's called 'Quick Swing.'"

There's another pitching machine at Teresa's parents' house. "Everywhere they went, they hit," Jake Jr. said.

When weather allowed, Jake III and Bill would take Joe into the backyard for games of Wiffle ball. Or they'd walk to Cretin to use the high school diamonds, or over to Griggs playground for an all-day smorgasbord of hockey, basketball, football and baseball.

Blessed with a big, powerful body and all that round-the-clock training, Joe would become perhaps the best all-around high school athlete in Minnesota history. He could be a quarterback at Florida State or

Cretin–Derham Hall quarterback Joe Mauer works on passing plays during practice in August 2000.

a basketball player at Minnesota, but the Twins, in their intensive research of him, discovered what Joe now readily admits.

"It was always baseball for me," he said. "This is what I always wanted to do."

Three strikes

For all of his athletic ability and familial advantages, Mauer had three strikes against him becoming the first pick in baseball's amateur draft—the first choice of millions of baseball-playing kids. He was a catcher—a difficult position to play, or for a scout to project. He was a high school player—a riskier proposition than a polished college athlete. And he was from Minnesota, meaning he played a fraction of the high school games of a player from California or Florida.

That is the negative way to look at Mauer. The Twins took a different view.

They saw the rarest of players—a left-handed-swinging, power-hitting, dart-throwing catcher from a good family who had proved himself as not only an elite baseball player in international competition but as an elite all-around athlete who never showed the strain of high expectations.

In short: Good catchers are hard to find. Catchers with Mauer's promise are rare as snow emergency parking signs in Fort Myers.

"He established himself, with his physical ability and size and body and general makeup [personality], that he could be one of the top guys in the draft," said Mike Radcliff, Twins scouting director. "Now what separates the top guy from the other top four or five is that we spent so much time with Joe, and watching Joe, that we felt we knew that he could handle pressure, could handle whatever gets thrown at him.

"We saw it in so many different venues—basketball, football, baseball. It's something we shook our heads at. I think the unbelievable baseball and sports background he and his family had, and the passion they all have for the game, I guess that's the only way you can try to figure out how he got to where he is, as far as being that advanced when coming from a non-hotbed area."

How rare is Mauer? The last time a high school catcher became the first pick in the draft was 1971, when the White Sox took Danny Goodwin of Peoria, Illinois.

Recruiting expert Tom Lemming compared Mauer as a prospect to a young Ken Griffey Jr., calling Mauer "one of the two most talented baseball seniors I've seen. I didn't see a player in football or baseball this year who had more potential."

Mauer led Cretin to the Class 3A state baseball championship while hitting .605 with nine doubles, seven triples, 15 homers, and 53 RBI. His cumulative high school average was .567 with one strikeout in 222 career at-bats. (The same year, Jake helped St. Thomas to the NCAA Division III championship with a .449 average and a team-record 84 hits.)

Joe became the first individual to be named the top player in two sports (football and baseball) by *USA Today* and was Gatorade and Parade football player of the year.

"I don't want to sound negative, but I don't think Joe can stack up to a Griffey or an Alex Rodriguez physically at this stage," Radcliff said. "Not when you consider running and throwing and all the physical tools. But in terms of skills, yeah, he's right there, because he is an advanced hitter, an advanced thrower, a fairly advanced catcher with good hands. Skills-wise he's a top-shelf guy."

That's why Radcliff dispenses with every scout's typical caution when projecting how quickly Mauer could move through the minors. "I'm probably a little more positive than I think our organization would be used to," Radcliff said. "We're usually more staid or conservative. I see no reason why Joe won't progress much faster than a normal high school catcher, or a normal high school first-rounder. His skills are just so advanced, and he has such a mature makeup.

"It takes 4.8 years for a normal high school guy to make it. I have every confidence Joe will be on a faster track than that."

Keeping score

Joe is happy with his dual residency. His parents' house is 10 minutes from the Metrodome and walking distance to Cretin; his new "bachelor pad," as Teresa calls it, is two minutes from the Twins' complex in Fort Myers and 10 minutes from the beach.

Joe and Jake III have developed a routine in Fort Myers. They get to the Twins' facility at 10 AM, play catch and pitch to each other, eat lunch, hit the gym, then finish the day with golf or tennis. Something that requires keeping score.

"We're still real competitive in just about everything," Joe said. "Last night we were playing tennis, and we've been going at it in golf."

The brothers admit they're tied, three matches each, in tennis. "It's written on the wall at home," Joe says. "We play video games, too, but it's usually something physical."

Jake delights in revealing that he beat Joe in golf the other day, "even though I've got my $80 starter-set irons, and he's got clubs so expensive they ought to swing themselves."

"We've always loved competing with each other," Jake said. "And Bill's coming down here in a couple of weeks. Then the competition will really pick up."

Jake knows the odds against him becoming a major league player are a little longer than those facing Joe. He's hardly jealous. "One of the reasons I wanted to go to school locally was so I could watch Joe's career," Jake said. "Now I can see myself kind of turn-

ing into Dad. Even today, during batting practice, I was just trying to throw to a spot where he needs work, keep throwing there to make him improve. I could hear myself making comments that Dad would say."

The brothers remember their parents stewing in the stands during games. "Then we'd hear about it on the car ride home," Joe says, laughing.

Said Jake: "I remember one time Bill missed a squeeze, and Dad got on him, and when he went out to the mound for the next inning, tears were running down Bill's face."

The brothers say their parents never embarrassed them, just "corrected them."

"They're coming down here for spring training, with a lot of other family members," Joe said. "I'm sure we'll hear about whatever we do wrong in the games."

Teresa makes no apologies. "Competition is not a bad word in our house," she said. "You have to compete in the real world, whether you're in business or sports or school. We tried never to get on them during games…but sometimes you'd just have to get up and take a walk."

She said she can remember disciplining Joe once—when he came home 26 minutes after curfew. His punishment: 26 days of doing dishes. "She knows I hate that, so it was a punishment that really worked," Joe said. "I was never late again."

On this brilliant December day, Jake and Joe are daring to ponder an uncertain future. If the Twins exist and if they both make it to the majors, they someday could position themselves 100 feet apart while playing for their hometown team.

"I do think it would be pretty neat to be wearing a Twins uniform, and throw out a runner—to my brother," Joe said.

Jake Jr. found that dream incomplete, saying, "We'd have to have Billy coming out of the bullpen." ●

A Year to Remember

Highlights of Joe Mauer's career senior year at Cretin–Derham Hall and 2001

November 3: Mauer ties a state record with seven touchdown passes in the Raiders' 62-34 victory over Eagan in the section playoffs. He is 16-for-21 for 337 yards in the three quarters he plays.

November 23: Mauer is named the *Star Tribune's* Metro Player of the Year in football and the Associated Press' state Player of the Year.

November 24: Eden Prairie defeats Cretin–Derham Hall 24–14 in the Class 5A football title game of the Prep Bowl. Mauer, who led the Raiders to the state title the season before, has an off day. He completes only 14 of 32 passes for 160 yards. He throws no touchdown passes and two interceptions.

December 7: Mauer is named the Gatorade Player of the Year in football, one of a handful of national awards he receives in this sport.

February 1: Mauer picks Florida State as his college choice for football over Arizona, Miami, and Minnesota.

February 8: On the first day of the national signing period in football, Mauer signs with Florida State.

March 20: Mauer, a 6-4 guard, is named to the *Star Tribune's* All-Metro first team in basketball.

March 22: In the semifinals of Class 4A state basketball tournament, Mauer scores a team-high 25 points and also has eight rebounds and five assists, but Cretin–Derham Hall loses 88–82 to Osseo, the eventual state champion. The Raiders take third place two days later.

May 17: Mauer homers in his seventh consecutive game—two shy of the national record—as the Raiders beat St. Paul Highland Park 10–0 in six innings. The streak ends the next game, when his only extra-base hit is a double.

May 24: Mauer hits for the cycle—and has a second triple—as Cretin–Derham Hall routs Minneapolis Washburn 20–0 in five innings at the Metrodome. Mauer finishes the regular season with a .625 average, 14 homers, and 48 RBI.

June 5: The Twins choose Mauer with the No. 1 pick in the major league amateur draft. That night, he goes 4-for-4 with a triple and two doubles as Cretin–Derham Hall defeats Woodbury 13–3 in five innings for a spot in the Class 3A state tournament field.

June 14: Mauer is named the *Star Tribune's* Metro Player of the Year in baseball, then has one of his best games of the season. He hits a game-tying three-run homer in the fifth inning and pitches five scoreless innings in relief as the Raiders beat Brainerd 5–4 in the Class 3A state semifinals. Mauer gives up one hit in his longest pitching outing of the season and strikes out nine.

June 15: Mauer goes 3-for-3 as Cretin–Derham Hall beats Rochester Mayo 13–2 in five innings at Midway Stadium for the Class 3A state baseball title. The Raiders finish 26–1 when Mauer catches a pop-up at first base for the game's last out.

July 17: Mauer signs a contract with the Twins; he receives a $5.15 million signing bonus to be paid over five years.

July 23: Mauer plays in his first professional game, with the Elizabethton Twins, and goes 2-for-4 as the DH. Both hits are singles.

August 31: After going 6-for-12 with a home run and five RBIs in Elizabethton's three-game playoff series, Mauer finishes his first summer of pro baseball with a .410 average in the rookie Appalachian League.

The Last Days Before the Draft

Scouts get final glances at Mauer

Patrick Reusse • May 26, 2001

The assessment of professional potential in young athletes is a difficult task in football, hockey and baseball. NFL scouts have the advantage of making decisions based on college competition. NHL scouts make most of their judgments based on watching players in what amount to semi-pro junior leagues and all-star settings.

When it comes to talent evaluation, there's no tougher job than trying to determine the future for a high school baseball player. This is particularly true in a northern climate, where weather greatly limits the schedule and the level of competition is marginal—compared with Florida, Arizona, Texas, or Southern California.

Some of baseball's best evaluators have visited Minnesota during this wet, ugly spring in order to get a final look at Joe Mauer, the Cretin–Derham Hall catcher. These scouts had the advantage of watching Mauer rip line drives for a national junior team last summer, so his standing as an elite prospect was assured.

There remained an obligation for the evaluators to inspect Mauer again this spring—to make sure the left handed swing and right handed throwing were as impressive as last summer.

Problem is, the scouts journey to this forsaken land, and they might have to wait four days for the monsoon to end and see a game played. Then, odds are they will see Mauer facing 75-miles-per-hour fastballs, most of which are not close to the plate.

On May 24, Cretin–Derham Hall was playing Washburn at the Metrodome. The Twins have the first selection in this draft, based on compiling the worst record in the American League in 2000. General manager Terry Ryan and other Twins' officials made the short walk from their offices to watch Mauer.

Officially, Mauer was 5-for-5—home run, two triples, double, and single—with eight RBIs. This was high school scorekeeping. Mauer was credited with a double when the Washburn right fielder dropped a fly ball. His first triple included an extra base when the ball was double-dribbled, also in right field.

The *Star Tribune's* stringent scorekeeping stance had Mauer going 4-for-5—still with a cycle of a single, double, triple, and home run, and still with eight RBIs. The home run carried over the Hefty bag in right-center by a yard; his 11th in the past 10 games.

There was one reason to temper the platitudes for this latest Mauer display: It was little more than batting practice, since Washburn was saving its better pitchers for the sectional tournament.

Then again, the five swings Mauer took were

Joe Mauer watching one of his five hits against Minneapolis Washburn. He hit for the cycle and then some that evening while knocking in 8 RBIs.

impressive, even by batting practice standards. It has been like this for Mauer all spring—to the point that *Baseball America,* the source that spends more time evaluating the draft than any other, now has him rated as the number one high school player in the country.

On the basis of talent, the magazine's draft issue will list the players thusly:

1) **Mark Prior, pitcher, Southern Cal;**
2) **Mark Teixeira, third baseman, Georgia Tech;**
3) **Joe Mauer;**
4) **Gavin Floyd, a high school pitcher from Maryland;**
5) **Dewon Brazelton, pitcher, Middle Tennessee State.**

The magazine also will have its mock draft. There, they will project that the Twins will take Mauer, followed by the Cubs taking Prior, then Brazelton to Tampa Bay, Floyd to Philadelphia, and Teixeira to Texas. ●

(opposite) Joe Mauer and the rest of the Cretin team take the field in the first inning of the 2001 Class 3A, Section 3 championship game vs. Woodbury at Midway Field in St. Paul. (above) A brand new graduate, Mauer waves to his family from the steps of the cathedral following Cretin–Derham Hall's commencement ceremony.

Draft Day

Homegrown kid is the No. 1 pick

Roman Augustoviz • June 6, 2001

After another important Cretin–Derham Hall baseball victory, Joe Mauer was asked if June 5, 2001, was the biggest day of his life. "So far," he said. It started at 10:30 AM when his mother, Teresa, woke him up to help clean the house before 25 to 30 family friends and Mauer's teammates in three varsity sports arrived. Shortly after noon, the Twins made the 18-year-old catcher the number one pick in the amateur baseball draft.

"Right now I'm excited to get picked," he said at a hastily called 2 PM news conference at his Catholic high school. "It's a dream come true.… But all I want to do is concentrate on my game tonight."

He refocused quite nicely.

Mauer went 4-for-4 with a triple, two doubles, and a single as the Raiders (23–1) routed Woodbury 13–3 in five innings at Midway Stadium in St. Paul to win the Class 3A, Section 3 title.

Mauer, a smooth-swinging, left-handed hitter who throws right handed, nearly hit for the cycle against Woodbury. His second double bounced off the fence in left-center. He had two RBIs and also threw out a runner trying to steal. "This is like a fairy tale," Mauer said. "I can't ask for anything better. It was a fun-filled day."

Oh, maybe one more thing.

The Mauers are hoping Joe's oldest brother, Jake III, a senior second baseman for NCAA Division III champion St. Thomas gets drafted, too. Another brother, Billy, pitched for North Hennepin Community College this spring. His father, Jake Jr., coaches all three on a summer adult men's team, so it's a real baseball family.

"My dad said my life has changed forever today," Joe Mauer said.

Having a game to play, Mauer said, helped him deal with all the pandemonium around him: "It's fun being out there. Sometimes fans give you heat, but that's OK. I feel at home out there."

At his real St. Paul home, everyone was clapping and cheering when an East Coast friend tipped the Mauers off on Joe's selection. Soon Twins General Manager Terry Ryan was calling to confirm the pick; he talked to Jack Jr.

"I was crying and hugging," Teresa said. "And I think I saw tears in Joe's eyes." Ryan and several members of his scouting staff were at the Mauer home for an hour the night before during the Twins game, but they made no guarantees. Joe slept soundly after the discussions.

"Nothing rattles him," Teresa Mauer said. "Sometimes I wonder if Joe has a pulse going. He is just so laid back. He doesn't get real excited or real down. He has always been that. He wants to play as hard as he can whether it's at Midway Stadium playing for a championship or in the backyard with his brothers." ●

The Twins had their eye on local product Joe Mauer since his youth, so it was no surprise when they drafted him.

CARLOS GONZALEZ

Lucky seven?

Joe Mauer became the seventh Minnesotan taken in the first round of Major League Baseball's amateur draft. Mauer is the first to be selected number one overall. Here's the complete list:

Year	Overall	Player
1969	13	Noel Jenke
1973	4	Dave Winfield
1977	3	Paul Molitor
1990	16	Dan Smith
1990	21	Tom Nevers
1993	18	Chris Schwab

The Mauer file

Joe Mauer's batting statistics in three seasons at Cretin–Derham Hall:

	Avg.	AB	H	2B	3B	HR	RBI	R	BB	K
Sophomore	.548	73	40	9	1	1	27	19	12	0
Junior	.542	59	32	8	4	5	31	28	12	1
Senior	.625	80	50	9	6	14	48	44	14	0
Career	.575	212	122	26	11	20	106	91	38	1

Note: As a junior, Mauer missed 10 games while playing with the U.S. junior national team. His run totals also include each time a courtesy runner scored for him; he used one every time he reached base his senior season except on home runs.

Mauers Double Their Pleasure

Mom thrilled Twins pick Jake

John Millea • June 7, 2001

Teresa Mauer was thrilled when her son Jake joined her son Joe as a Twins draft pick, and she will be absolutely giddy if they begin their pro careers as minor league teammates. But wherever her boys play, she will have to see for herself that everything is all right

"Moms never quit worrying," she said after a phone call from the Twins set off a celebration in the family's St. Paul home for the second day in a row. "It's given me a little more peace of mind, but I think I'm still going to have to go and check it out."

Jake, 22, a two-time NCAA Division III All-America second baseman who helped St. Thomas win a national title this year, was taken by the Twins with the first pick in the 23rd round, the 667th overall selection. Jake hit .391 in four seasons with the Tommies, who had a 154–42 record in that time. Jake also helped Cretin–Derham Hall win state titles in 1996 and 1997. Number one overall pick Joe Mauer, 18, is a senior catcher at Cretin, which will play in the state tournament.

"Joe was taken on his own merits," Twins general manager Terry Ryan said. "He's a good-looking hitter."

After the Twins called Wednesday, the brothers didn't need to say much to each other. "[Joe] just kind of smiled and gave me a hug," Jake said. "It was kind of unspoken."

The Mauers have been teammates only once, playing last summer on a team coached by their dad, also named Jake, in a St. Paul summer league. Their brother Bill also was on the team; he will be a junior pitcher at Concordia University in St. Paul in the fall.

The Twins would like the Mauers to begin their pro careers at rookie league Elizabethton, Tennessee. That team begins its season June 19. "That's where we speculate sending them," said Twins scouting director Mike Radcliff, adding that signing Jake should help in contract talks with Joe. "Automatically it's a factor, sure. They're brothers," he said. "But we had Jake on our board, too."

Jake said, "It would be kind of neat to play on the same team. Joe's real mature for his age, so I wouldn't have to do too much babysitting."

Every major league team had thoroughly scouted Joe Mauer, while Jake has had a quieter career. Jake, who doesn't have an agent, is 6'2", 175 pounds and Joe is 6'4", 215. All that matters now, however, is they both went to the Twins, even if they were 666 picks apart.

"It's been a great couple of days," Teresa said. "There had been some teams that were interested in Jake, and we were just crossing our fingers hoping the Twins would get him." ●

Joe Mauer and brother Jake stretch during warm-ups before a game while playing for the E-Town Twins in Elizabethton, Tennessee.

Star Attraction

Mauer makes his pro debut in Elizabethton, Tennessee

Chip Scoggins • July 24, 2001

With rock music blaring in the background, all eyes focused on No. 7 as he methodically went through his routine. Back and forth, he swung two wooden bats, one black, the other brown. The bright sun was disappearing behind him. Cameras clicked in the distance. Children screamed his name.

The kid went about his business, oblivious to it all. He adjusted his jersey, tightened his batting gloves, stretched his arms skyward, pushed down on his helmet until everything felt just right.

Seven weeks of anticipation and a lifetime of preparation led to this moment. Seven weeks of questions and contract deliberations: will he or won't he? baseball or football? In the end, baseball, he said, was always his first love.

And so seven weeks after the Twins made him the first pick in the Major League Baseball amateur draft, Joe Mauer made his professional debut for the Twins' rookie league team under the eager and watchful eyes of a baseball-crazed community that nearly burst at the seams awaiting his arrival.

In the bottom of the second inning, anticipation finally gave way to reality. "Ladies and gentlemen, let's give a big welcome to No. 7, the designated hitter, Joe Mauer," the voice boomed over the loudspeakers.

The crowd of 1,000 roared as Mauer dug into the batter's box. It took all of three pitches before the cheers turned to jeers. Pulaski (Virginia) Rangers pitcher Hayden Gardner started Mauer with three consecutive balls, none close, and the Elizabethton fans were seething. "Come on, pitch to him," a man yelled over the boos. The catcalls grew louder after Gardner delivered ball four.

Mauer smoked a first-pitch fastball to center field in his second at-bat: a crisp single. Gardner tossed the ball to the Twins dugout, a keepsake for Mauer's collection. Mauer finished 2-for-4 on a pair of singles in a 7–5 loss. He struck out once, the same number he had in his record-setting high school career at Cretin–Derham Hall. But this is professional baseball, and Monday was a solid start to what Twins officials hope is a long, promising career.

"It's been pretty crazy since I got drafted," Mauer said. "I still kind of wonder if this is all really happening. I was kind of nervous that first at-bat. But it was great to get back out there and get the first game under my belt."

The first look

First impressions have great significance when you are the bonus baby and the ink is barely dry on your $5.15 million contract—the largest bonus afforded a Twins draft choice.

"Without a doubt, these have been the most active two or three days I have ever had here," Elizabethton general manager Mike Mains said. "It is so rare for something like this to happen. Everywhere I go in

Joe Mauer warms up before the start of a game in Elizabethton, which competes in the Appalachian League.

Joe Mauer makes a hard slide into home plate after a base hit in his first official at bat during his pro debut. Mauer walked on his first at bat and made it to third base but did not score.

town, people are talking about Joe. It's just been a wonderful experience for us and our town."

Fans arrived early Monday armed with pens, programs, hats, shirts—anything for Mauer to sign. A group of Little Leaguers competing in the state baseball tournament stood outside the clubhouse asking everyone who passed by if they had seen Joe "Morrow."

Elizabethton resident Scott Honeycutt didn't even try to pronounce Mauer's name, instead referring to him as "the big boy." "We had to come see him," Honeycutt said. "We're expecting big things from him. But that's a lot of pressure for a young kid. It's pretty neat to have him here."

It also is a new experience for Mauer's teammates. Many said they were surprised at how unassuming and soft-spoken he is. They tease him about his celebrity and marvel at his hitting skills.

"I heard he was a legend in Minnesota," pitcher Jason Miller said. "Heard he can't walk down the street without someone recognizing him."

Mauer's teammates appeared starstruck when he stepped into the batting cage hours after joining the team Saturday. Everyone—coaches, players, team officials—came to a standstill and watched.

"Guys came out of the clubhouse to watch him hit," said outfielder Barry Quickstad, a native of Waseca, Minnesota. "Everyone was excited to see him."

The euphoria should subside now that Mauer has played his first game. Former Twins catcher Ray Smith, who is Elizabethton's hitting coach, said Mauer will be handled wisely but not differently. "We're not going to do anything stupid, but he will do the same things as everyone else," Smith said. "He is a member of a team and organization now. We're going to expect just as much out of him as the rest of the guys."

Just an ordinary Joe? If that were only the case. ●

The Future, the Lock

Joe Maurer makes his debut

Jim Souhan • April 4, 2004

I t would be easy to call him The Natural if the position he plays weren't the most unnatural in sport. Joe Mauer might be the best athlete in Minnesota high school history and one of the best prospects in recent baseball history. His reward for such excellence: squatting like a frog, taking foul tips off his elbows, and spending more time talking adults through crises than Dr. Phil.

Mauer will make his big-league debut in his home state, playing for the team he cheered for as a child, while his family fills a section of the Metrodome. Before he drinks his first legal beer, Mauer, 20, will fulfill a childhood dream while playing a position that requires more maturity and pain tolerance than parenthood.

Rookie catcher? That's baseball's oxymoronic equivalent to "jumbo shrimp."

"It's the toughest position to break in at," Angels manager and former Dodgers catcher Mike Scioscia said. "You have to know so much. The 140 pitches you call will have more chance of deciding the game than anything else you do, even if you hit two home runs."

In the past 40 years, only four 20-year-olds have become everyday catchers—Johnny Bench, Ivan Rodriguez, Butch Wynegar, and Bob Didier. A larger percentage of the population has won the lottery.

Bench is in the Hall of Fame. Rodriguez might be on his way. Wynegar was a phenom hampered by injuries. Didier had a short, modest career.

Mauer's pedigree and skills suggest he'll spend more time being compared to a Bench than sitting on one. The raves of scouts, teammates, and coaches indicate the kid from Cretin–Derham Hall might be embarking on a career stuffed with Gold Gloves, All-Star Games, and Metrodome family reunions.

"That's a rare guy right there," Twins center fielder Torii Hunter said. "He's 20, but he's 20 going on 40. To take pitches like he does, to throw out people the way he does, to call games like he does, and to do it all with that personality and character, that's special.

"He got me a drink of water the other day. I'm like, 'What? A first-round draft pick getting me water?' Most of those guys have too much testosterone and ego to do that. He's going to be one of my soul brothers."

Not that Mauer needs any more relatives. This winter and spring he roomed with brothers Billy and Jake at his Fort Myers condo and returned from spring training games to find the place overflowing with aunts, uncles, nephews, nieces, and grandparents.

"My parents have helped me out," Mauer said. "They've warned people, 'He needs to get his rest.'

Joe Mauer heads to first base after taking four balls from then-Cleveland Indians pitcher CC Sabathia.

Everybody wants to go out to dinner every night, but some nights I just have to stay in."

That doesn't exactly cramp Mauer's style. If he were a color, he would be beige. If he were an amusement park ride, he would be a monorail.

"He doesn't say much," Jake said. "But he really doesn't have to."

Not when you strike out once in your high school career, become an All-America in football and baseball, and a potential Division I recruit in basketball, spurn the quarterback job at Florida State to sign with your hometown baseball team, hit a combined .330 in 277 minor league games, be proclaimed the game's top prospect by Baseball America, then prompt the trade of an All-Star catcher.

Mauer will play a difficult position under difficult circumstances—replacing A.J. Pierzynski, one of the most valuable Twins of recent vintage.

"Joe will handle it fine," Pierzynski said. "He's so mature. The tough thing about the position is you'll go through stretches where nothing goes right, and it's not like you're an outfielder who can practice his swing between pitches. You've got to worry about everything that happens on the field.

"The pitching staff really counts on you. I just hope he doesn't get stretched too thin off the field by family and friends and distractions. He's going to hit for average because of that great swing. I don't know if he's going to hit for power for a while.

"People need to be patient, but there's no doubt he'll be good."

Super Joe

On a recent morning in the dugout, a bunch of players wondered about Mauer's decision to sign with the Twins for $5 million rather than play quarterback at

Florida State. "Hey, Super Joe," outfielder Jacque Jones said. "How much money would you have made at Florida State?"

Mauer smiled. "I'm not supposed to talk about that," he said.

He's usually content to let others do the talking. Here's what they're saying:

First baseman Doug Mientkiewicz: "He's a great guy, and the best thing about him is you know he's not going to change. He's already had enough fame and attention. He is who he is."

Hitting coach Scott Ullger: "He's unbelievable. The other night he backhanded a pitch in the dirt and threw a guy out by 5 feet. Most catchers would be happy just to block it, and he made it look like a pitchout. He has a lot to learn. But there's no doubt he'll learn it."

Fellow Cretin alum and Mariners hitting coach Paul Molitor: "Young players are more susceptible to the ups and downs of the game. That's where Joe has an edge, because he's not an overaggressive guy at the plate, he knows the strike zone, and he's so mechanically sound defensively that he was never going to embarrass himself at any level, at any stage of his life.

"He is so introverted that he's going to have to assume more of a vocal role and gain the respect of his pitchers. You know how talented he is and what a great head he has on his shoulders, so you expect more from him than most 20-year-olds."

The sweetest swing

Ullger said Mauer has the best swing in camp. And he said that two years ago, when Mauer was 18. Scouts

in Florida and Arizona said Mauer will be the best defensive catcher in baseball. Not in 2005. In April.

His teammates say he might not produce much power immediately and might have to learn how to battle through the first extended slumps of his career but that there is no doubting his prowess.

A reporter mentioned Pierzynski to Twins outfielder Mike Ryan. He changed the subject. "Mauer's awesome," he said. "The total package. I've never seen a swing like that. He's exceptional behind the plate, and he can hit anything. It's a pleasure just to watch him."

And yet the Twins know they'll have to watch him. If he were a fleet center fielder or a power-hitting first baseman, Mauer might be able to survive on raw talent. Hitting a 95-mile-per-hour fastball requires skill and technique that Mauer already possesses. Calling pitches against the Yankees requires knowledge and savvy.

"Catching is a total feel thing," Scioscia said. "It's not a push-button operation. It's the last thing that really develops in a catcher, and it's a constant state of evolution, because you're always working with new pitchers against different hitters.

"There's going to be a lot of focus on that, because he's breaking in with a team that won two divisions in a row. What wins games at the major league level is calling a good game. There's no substitute for experience."

Scioscia's theory is that a catcher needs at least 500 minor league games to prepare for the big leagues. Mauer has played 277—and just 73 above Class A. Mauer's backup, Henry Blanco, played in 963 minor league games before making it to the majors.

So why do the Twins, from GM Terry Ryan to Gardenhire to Pierzynski's buddy Mientkiewicz, rave

JEFF WHEELER

JEFF WHEELER

about a kid who could so easily inspire jealousy or doubt?

"He knows the game," Twins pitcher Carlos Silva said.

"A pitcher missed a sign the other day, and Joe ran out there and corrected him," Gardenhire said. "The kid's 20, and he's taking charge. That's pretty good."

"He works at it," Mientkiewicz said. "He sticks around and watches the whole game, instead of coming into the clubhouse and messing around with us, which is great. He needs to watch, and he does."

"He's easy to pitch to, he provides a good target, works well with pitchers, and he's quick to learn," Ryan said. "When you tell him something, you don't have to tell him twice."

"Joe did the same thing Wynegar did," former Twins pitcher Bert Blyleven said. "He got so low behind the plate, which really helps the pitchers, and he moves left and right with such ease.

"What has impressed me the most out of Joe is how calm he is. Butch was the same way—very sure of himself, but not overconfident. What's going to help

Joe is he's got good pitchers to work with."

Wynegar broke in with the Twins in 1976, under manager Gene Mauch. He hit .260 with 10 homers and 69 RBI in 149 games.

"I started off slow in April," said Wynegar, now the Brewers hitting coach. "It wasn't until I hit my first home run off Catfish Hunter in New York and came home and hit one off Jim Palmer that I felt like I belonged. So much was put on the defensive side of things that I took me a while to get my hitting going. Gene was very supportive. That really helped."

The Mauer Shift?

The other day Mauer faced reigning Cy Young Award winner Roy Halladay, and something unexpected happened. The Blue Jays used a defensive shift—against a kid out of Class AA. They pushed their infielders and outfielders toward the left-field line, hoping to take advantage of Mauer's natural, opposite-field swing. "They did that to me in Double-A, too," Mauer said.

So Mauer took an outside fastball and hit a shot, foul, down the left-field line. Then he took a fastball that got a bit more of the plate and lined it up the middle for a single.

In his next at-bat, Halladay tried to throw a cut fastball on the inside corner, and Mauer yanked it to right for a single. "He does those kinds of things all the time," Ullger said. "You start to expect the unbelievable from him.

"As a hitter, he adjusts so quickly. And throwing batting practice to him is a pleasure. It's like you draw it up—he hits outside pitches to the opposite field, drops the bat head and turns on the inside pitch, and everything he hits has that backspin you want."

Twins Rookies: Ones to Remember

• **Tony Oliva, 1964:** Had one of baseball's greatest rookie seasons, claiming the AL batting title with a .323 average while adding 32 home runs and 94 RBIs.

• **Rod Carew, 1967:** Owner Calvin Griffith ordered manager Sam Mele to start Carew at second base. One season removed from Class A, Carew batted .292.

• **Kent Hrbek, 1982:** Classic story of hometown boy making good. The Bloomington Kennedy product batted .301 with 23 HR and 92 RBIs, finishing second to Cal Ripken Jr. for AL Rookie of the Year.

• **Kirby Puckett, 1984:** Summoned to the Twins on May 8, he had to borrow $80 for cab fare to the game in Anaheim. He had four hits that night and batted .296 overall.

• **Chuck Knoblauch, 1991:** A Texas A&M All-America, he was 22 and short of two seasons in the minors when he batted .281 with 25 stolen bases, helping the Twins to the World Series championship.

Twins Rookies of the Year

Tony Oliva, 1964: .323, 32 HR, 94 RBI
Rod Carew, 1967: .292, 66 runs, 51 RBI
John Castino, 1979: .285, 5 HR, 52 RBI
Chuck Knoblauch, 1991: .281, 78 runs, 25 SB
Marty Cordova, 1995: .277, 24 HR, 84 RBI

Thrown Into the Fire

In the past 40 years, four players have become everyday catchers at the age of 20. Here's how they fared in their first full season (Johnny Bench played 26 games the previous year):

Player	Yr.	Games	AB	2B	3B	HR	RBI	Avg.
Butch Wynegar	1976	149	534	21	2	10	69	.260
Ivan Rodriguez	1991	88	280	16	0	3	27	.264
Johnny Bench	1968	154	564	40	2	15	82	.275
Bob Didier	1969	114	352	16	1	0	32	.256

Realistic expectations

An informal survey of scouts, players and coaches produced this consensus: Mauer can be expected to hit .280 or better with gap power and a high on-base percentage, while instantly becoming one of baseball's best defensive catchers.

"We've tried to downplay expectations, but he's a phenomenon," Gardenhire said. "You sign autographs, and all the fans want to know is, 'Is Joe playing today?' You can't expect too much from a 20-year-old, but we all know what's waiting for him down the road."

"We can't pump up expectations to the point where if he doesn't hit .340, people are disappointed," Mientkiewicz said. "He'll be just fine, but he's going to strike out more than once. This isn't high school.

"The other day he struck out and came back to the dugout saying, 'I feel like there's a hole in my bat. I thought I was going to hit it, and I completely missed.' And I'm like, 'Welcome to the big leagues.'"

Ask Mauer about the imminent challenge, and he says, "I'm looking forward to it."

What was his biggest previous challenge?

"When I was 16, I played on an 18-year-old team at the world championships in Taiwan," he said. "I lost about 10 pounds, because I couldn't eat the food, and the competition was unbelievable."

And? "We won the gold," he said.

Of course.

"It's a tough job, being a catcher at a young age," Royals manager and former catcher Tony Pena said. "But Pudge [Ivan Rodriguez] was pretty young, wasn't he? And he was pretty good."

Bullpen coach Rick Stelmaszek is the Twins' longest-tenured uniformed employee. He caught for the Washington Senators, California Angels, Texas Rangers, and Chicago Cubs and spent a spring playing for Ted Williams.

He might be the Twin least prone to hype anyone.

"Joe's going to have to deal with double-deck syndrome—playing in these big ballparks for the first time," Stelmaszek said. "He's going to have to learn to call a game, to work with our pitchers, to deal with slumps."

Early in camp, pitching prospect J.D. Durbin established himself as a character befitting his nickname—"The Real Deal."

"That nickname of Durbin's? He needs to give it up," Stelmaszek said. "Because this kid Mauer, he's the one who's 'The Real Deal.'" ●

The M&M Boys

Joe Mauer and Justin Morneau officially hold the keys to the Twins' future

Joe Christensen • April 2, 2005

Heading into a season that rests heavily on their young shoulders, Twins sluggers Joe Mauer and Justin Morneau would love to tell you what it's like to hit together in the same lineup. But there's one problem: It has never happened. Outside of spring training and the 2001 fall instructional league, where none of the results counted, Mauer and Morneau have never played in the same game.

It's almost uncanny, really, because the Twins' talent evaluators had visions of everything working out this way from the start. From the moment they laid eyes on Mauer, they saw a prototypical No. 3 hitter, just as they saw a prototypical cleanup hitter in Morneau.

The two soft-spoken giants—each standing 6-4 and swinging a left-handed stick—became the crown jewels of a thriving farm system. Now, after winning three consecutive division titles, the Twins are ready to let these two children of the 1980s anchor their starting lineup.

Batting third: the 21-year-old Mauer. Batting fourth: the 23-year-old Morneau. Combined major league experience: 149 games.

But even under that pressure at their age, they have carried themselves with a quiet confidence that has endeared them to the team's veterans. Spend two weeks in the team's clubhouse, and you barely hear them make a sound.

"Both of those guys came up with no chips on their shoulder, no cockiness—it was all respect," Twins center fielder Torii Hunter said. "And as far as hitters go, these guys are 10 times better than I was when I came in."

Twins general manager Terry Ryan spoke a bit more cautiously, especially at the suggestion that Mauer and Morneau could become the Twins' own version of the M&M Boys, like the Yankees once had with Mickey Mantle and Roger Maris. "It's a little premature to anoint both of these guys All-Star-type players, until they get a track record," Ryan said. "But they're capable of being very good players at the major league level."

Groomed for stardom

For Mauer, those expectations have been there for years. Born in St. Paul on April 19, 1983, he became a three-sport star at Cretin–Derham Hall and turned down a scholarship to play quarterback at Florida State after the Twins made him the first overall pick in the 2001 draft.

Mauer became so good so fast that the Twins made room by trading former All-Star catcher A.J. Pierzynski. By last year at this time, every decision the

Joe Mauer and first baseman Justin Morneau seemingly swing in synchronization while loosening up during a Twins game against the Detroit Tigers at the Metrodome.

CARLOS GONZALEZ

ELIZABETH FLORES

Twins had ever made about Mauer—from the Pierzynski trade, to letting Mauer jump from Class AA to the big leagues, to picking him ahead of Mark Prior in the draft—looked brilliant.

Mauer dazzled the scouts last spring, offensively and defensively, and the Twins couldn't wait to unveil him as their starting catcher. But their euphoria was soon dashed. In the season's second game, Mauer went back to catch a foul ball and wrenched his left knee.

He had surgery, returned to action for six weeks, and then had to shut it down again in mid-July. It was a terribly frustrating ordeal, but there was the promise of a healthy return for 2005. In 35 games, Mauer had left a sample-size record showing his potential—batting .308 with six home runs and 17 RBI—that only left the organization hungry for more.

Talk to Twins officials about Mauer and Morneau these days, and it's tough to keep them focused on both subjects. Inevitably, their thoughts shift directly to Mauer.

Even Morneau gushes: "He doesn't hit like he's 21 years old. The way he takes pitches. That quiet confidence he has. It's a confidence, not a cockiness. It's like he knows something we don't know."

The ringmaster

While Mauer's every move was chronicled through the minor leagues, Morneau's rise has had its jaw-dropping moments, too. He was born on May 16, 1981, and played goalie in hockey growing up in New Westminster, British Columbia. The Twins drafted him as a catcher in 1999 with their third-round pick

"He was one of those guys who kind of gained steam in the draft room," said Rob Anthony, Twins director of baseball operations.

After at first considering Morneau a lower-round pick, the Twins decided they couldn't pass on his power potential. Before long, they were thanking their lucky stars for that decision. He signed his contract and donned a Twins uniform for a ceremonial batting practice at the Metrodome.

At age 18, swinging a wooden bat instead of aluminum, Morneau began launching balls into the right field upper deck. Anthony called it the most amazing batting practice display he'd ever seen from a draft pick.

"I hit one ball off the facing [of the upper deck] and just kind of relaxed," Morneau said.

With concerns about Morneau's throwing arm, the Twins converted him from a catcher into a first baseman. His defense was suspect, but not his bat. He helped teams at three minor league levels win championships. "It was a standing joke with the managers," Twins minor league director Jim Rantz said. "They said, 'Hey, send this kid Morneau for the playoffs because we want to get a ring.'"

Growing pains

Thrilled with Morneau's power, the Twins cleared a permanent spot for him last July by trading popular

The Justin Morneau File

Height: 6-4, Wt.: 227
Drafted: third round in June 1999
2004 stats: .271, 19 HR, 58 RBI

He'll be a star because: He has a powerful swing and already has shown for half a season that he can thrive in the big leagues. Besides hitting home runs, he also hit for a high average in the minors.

The concern: He hit .240 with three home runs in 75 at-bats against left-handed pitchers and .283 with 16 homers in 205 at-bats against right-handers.

Betcha didn't know: Morneau was drafted as a catcher. He's not as good defensively as former Twins first baseman Doug Mientkiewicz, but Mientkiewicz said this spring that Morneau is better at the position than most people think.

Mauer on Morneau: "It's pretty good to have a guy hitting behind you who can leave the park any time. That's a big bat you've got to worry about."

first baseman Doug Mientkiewicz to the Boston Red Sox. In a little less than a half-season, Morneau hit .271 with 19 home runs and 58 RBIs.

But even in a season that saw Mauer establish himself as the team's best No. 3 hitter and Morneau as its best cleanup hitter, Twins manager Ron Gardenhire never wrote their names into the same lineup. Morneau played all 74 of his games with Mauer out because of the left knee injury. They kept missing each other, just as they had through the minor leagues.

Morneau, who came up from Class AAA for a brief

ELIZABETH FLORES

Double Trouble

Tho Twins have had several pairings and groups of young players that have helped usher in different eras of success. Joe Mauer and Justin Morneau are just the latest twosome to have the hope of the franchise rest on their big, strong shoulders. Here's a look back at their debut seasons:

1961—Harmon Killebrew and Bob Allison

Killebrew, destined for the Hall of Fame, was in his prime at the start of a decade where he'd be one of baseball's most feared sluggers. Allison hit 247 home runs during a 10-year span, starting in 1959.

1961	Age	Bats	Avg.	HR	RBI
Harmon Killebrew	25	R	.288	46	122
Bob Allison	26	R	.245	29	105

1984—Kirby Puckett and Kent Hrbek

Puckett joined the Twins after the season started; within two years the "singles hitter" would become a slugger, with 31 home runs. Hrbek had his best season in 1984. He finished with 293 home runs in his 14-year career.

1984	Age	Bats	Avg.	HR	RBI
Kirby Puckett	23	R	.296	0	31
Kent Hrbek	24	L	.311	27	107

2000—Torii Hunter and Jacque Jones

First noted for speed and defensive prowess, Hunter and Jones provided pop in the lineup during three consecutive AL Central title seasons. Hunter has 105 homers in the past four seasons; Jones has 100 over the past five.

2000	Age	Bats	Avg.	HR	RBI
Torii Hunter	24	R	.280	5	44
Jacque Jones	25	L	.285	19	76

stint in May while Mauer was out, returned to the majors for good on July 16. Mauer had played his last game one day earlier. They were two prospects passing in the night, but they stayed close, with a friendship that dates to their time together in the fall instructional league.

In fact, Mauer had an extra bedroom at his St. Paul apartment last year, so Morneau crashed there for a while. They were roommates but never lineup mates. "Our goal now," Morneau said, "is to stay healthy all year."

It won't be easy. Mauer's left knee flared up again in early March, and he missed another week because of a gum infection. How much he'll catch this season remains to be seen. It could be just three or four times a week, with another couple of games spent as the designated hitter.

Then there's Morneau. His offseason could have been dedicated to medical science. He had an appendectomy and dealt with chicken pox, pleurisy, and pneumonia. In March, he had minor surgery to have a lymph node removed.

At least the Twins can say this: Early in their careers, Mauer and Morneau have learned never to take their health for granted.

"I think we've both had everything you could possibly have," Mauer said.

First-time pairing

Ask anyone how good the Twins lineup will be with a healthy Mauer and Morneau, and it's pure speculation. "I like him hitting in front of me," Morneau said. "He gets on base. He sees a lot of pitches, so I can get a good read on the pitcher, and we can kind of feed off each other."

Said Mauer: "It's pretty good to have a guy hitting

The Joe Mauer File

Height.: 6-4, Wt.: 226
Drafted: first round (first overall) in June 2001
2004 stats: .308, 6 HR, 17 RBI

He'll be a star because: He has uncanny plate discipline and a swing that some have called "slump-proof." Defensively, he could become the best catcher in baseball.

The concern: A left knee injury limited him to 35 games last season, and the knee flared up once this spring. Some question how long a large man with a bad knee can keep catching.

Betcha didn't know: He has a two-bedroom apartment in St. Paul where teammates Justin Morneau, Jason Bartlett, Jason Kubel, Jesse Crain, and J.D. Durbin have stayed.

Morneau on Mauer: "It's a confidence, not a cockiness. It's like he knows something we don't know."

---

behind you who can leave the park [with a home run] any time. That's a big bat you've got to worry about."

Gardenhire said he thinks Mauer will eventually surprise people with his power, just as Morneau will surprise by hitting for a high average. But neither player has completed a full season in the big leagues, and therein lie the questions.

What happens when the Twins go through the inevitable team-wide offensive slumps? Will young players in crucial roles begin to press, instead of relaxing the way veteran players could?

Toronto Blue Jays general manager J.P. Ricciardi said it will help Mauer and Morneau that there will be experienced hitters such as Hunter, Jacque Jones, and

Joe Mauer celebrates a late-inning home run with teammate and friend Justin Morneau.

CARLOS GONZALEZ

JEFF WHEELER

Shannon Stewart in the lineup. "The Twins do such a good job putting players in a position to succeed," Ricciardi said. "I think [Mauer and Morneau] are going to be very good major league players for a long time."

Gardenhire and Ryan said they aren't overly concerned about Mauer and Morneau crumbling beneath the pressure.

In scouting terms, Mauer's compact swing, selective approach, and ability to spray the ball to all fields make him less susceptible to prolonged slumps. Morneau takes bigger, more aggressive cuts.

"He's going to strike out a little bit," Gardenhire said of Morneau, "but when he's staying within himself, he's a pretty good hitter."

With their pitching staff returning intact from last season, the Twins are hoping an improved offense will help take them deeper into the playoffs. Morneau and Mauer realize much of that burden now falls to them.

"If you don't have production from your 3-4 hitters, then you're not going to win," Morneau said. "Obviously there's a lot of pressure. But nobody's going to put more pressure on us than we already put on ourselves." ●

Fresh Expectations

A healthy Joe Mauer is geared up to show 2005's stats were low by his standards

Joe Christensen • February 21, 2006

The first good omen of spring training for the Twins didn't come on the freshly manicured fields of the Lee County Sports Complex. It came at Gator Lanes, the local alley where Joe Mauer recently bowled the game of his life.

True story: Manager Ron Gardenhire knows a guy there who equipped Mauer with a custom-made ball.

Mauer, a three-sport star from Cretin-Derham Hall, had never rolled anything better than a 150. But in his third game with the new ball...265. "It was unbelievable," Mauer said. "I had a strike the first frame. The second frame, I had a spare. And then I rolled eight strikes in a row. I didn't know what was going on."

Maybe it was a good sign. As their pitchers and catchers held their first workout Monday, the Twins could dare to dream of Mauer carrying that stunning success into the season.

At age 22, he is one of the first players mentioned when scouts are asked to name the sport's potential breakout stars for 2006. In 2005, the Twins were deeply concerned about Mauer's left knee. After a knee injury limited him to 35 games in 2004, Mauer went the distance in his second season in the big leagues, turning in a solid, if unspectacular, campaign. In 131 games, he hit .294 with nine home runs and 55 RBIs. Mauer said it was the worst he had performed at any level.

Of course, with his .324 career minor-league average and his otherworldly success from high school, he had established some lofty standards.

Several young Twins experienced the same letdown last year. Mauer, Justin Morneau, and others had done nothing but win all the way through their professional careers. "In this organization, you're used to winning," Mauer said. "Last year was a little different. But this year, I guess we're not the favorite in our division. That might take a lot of pressure off of guys, and I think we're going to surprise a lot of people."

Much of that will hinge on Mauer's progression as a hitter. His .372 on-base percentage led all Twins regulars by a wide margin last year. But some scouts say to take the next step, he needs to start jumping on inside pitches more and turn them into home runs.

Gardenhire disagrees, saying the team needs to let Mauer progress at his own rate. "Home runs are going to come." Gardenhire said. "He's pretty good. He has a pretty good plan."

Those comments show the level of respect and trust Mauer has gained within the organization, even two months shy of his 23rd birthday.

Twins officials let him decide if he wanted to play

in the World Baseball Classic. Mauer chose not to go, even though Team USA manager Buck Martinez had raved about the young catcher upon naming him to the provisional roster in January.

The next time the WBC is held, perhaps in four years, Mauer might reconsider. "Definitely," he said. "Any time you get a chance to represent your country, it's pretty awesome. It's just bad timing for me. If it's further down the road, and I've been through everything healthwise, I'd love to do it."

Mauer said the decision wasn't based solely on his knee. Last year pushed his entire body to new limits as he learned the rigors of being an everyday catcher in the big leagues. The schedule is longer, the games more intense.

He returned to spring training with a better understanding of what's in store for his body for the next

A Breakout Season of Puckett-like Proportions

When Twins officials talk about a possible breakout season for Joe Mauer, thoughts of Kirby Puckett invariably come to mind. Puckett, like Mauer this season, had one full major league season under his belt when he went to spring training in 1986. Here's a look at Puckett's 1985 season, and his breakout year the following summer.

Kirby Puckett	G	AB	R	H	2B	3B	HR	RBI	Avg.
1985	161	691	80	199	29	13	4	74	.288
1986	161	680	119	223	37	6	31	96	.328

Joe Mauer	G	AB	R	H	2B	3B	HR	RBI	Avg.
2005	131	489	61	144	26	2	9	55	.294

Class of 2001

A look at how the top five picks in the 2001 amateur draft have performed at the major league level:

Pick	Player	Team	2005 stats	Career stats
No. 1	Joe Mauer	Twins	.294, 9 HR, 55 RBI	.297, 15 HR, 72 RBI in 166 games
No. 2	Mark Prior	Cubs	11–7, 3.67 ERA	41–23, 3.24 in 97 starts
No. 3	Dewon Brazelton	Devil Rays	1–8, 7.61	8–23, 5.98 in 54 games (41 starts)
No. 4	Gavin Floyd	Phillies	1–2, 10.04	3–2, 6.63 in 13 games (8 starts)
No. 5	Mark Teixeira	Rangers	.301, 43 HR, 144 RBI	.282, 107 HR, 340 RBI in 453 games

seven months. He also returned to the same boring routine. Mauer has a house in Fort Myers, and his roommates this spring are his brother, Jake, and Twins minor-league pitcher J.D. Durbin.

Durbin and Mauer might seem like an odd couple, rooming together. But it speaks to the way Mauer's singular focus makes him a stabilizing force for the Twins. Once considered a hotshot prospect, Durbin has developed a reputation for being more flash than substance. He moved in with Mauer, a longtime minor-league teammate, hoping for a fresh start.

"I could have stayed somewhere else," Durbin said. "I had a rough year last year, and I'm kind of running out of options. I came to stay with Joe to be a little more level-headed."

When Mauer isn't at the ballpark, Durbin said, he's usually home watching TV. "He just likes to sit around," Durbin said. "The other day, I got so bored, I just started cleaning his house."

But that doesn't mean the group won't have any fun here in Florida. Mauer said he's determined to keep bowling once a week. ●

Joe Mauer left watches teammate Lew Ford during batting practice prior to their 2006 home opener against the Oakland Athletics.

Mauer's First All-Star Game

Joe Mauer is proving that all the hype was more than justified

La Velle E. Neal III • July 9, 2006

Joe Mauer is the youngest player in the Twins lineup. And their most polished hitter. "That patient at 23?" teammate Torii Hunter said. "He's one of the most impressive young guys to me, as far as hitting."

Imagine a fan turned on, its blade smoothly accelerating into motion. That's Mauer's swing. "Everyone wants to hit like that, but that's kind of hard," said roommate Justin Morneau, the Twins' powerful first baseman. "My swing is a little more violent."

Most impressive about Mauer is that the St. Paul native has simplified the dual challenge of catching and batting third, the most important spot in the order.

"He's a guy who could always hit but had to worry about other things," said Diamondbacks scout Al Newman, a former Twins coach. "Now, it is just flowing for him."

Mauer's major league-leading .388 batting average has earned him a spot in his first All-Star Game.

Can he do it at catcher?

The wear and tear on even hot-hitting catchers as the season wears on is well-documented: Mauer would be the first American League catcher to win a batting championship.

Mike Piazza had a .362 average and 201 hits in 1997 for the Dodgers; both are records for a catcher. Hall of Famer Bill Dickey hit .362 in 1936.

"They were talking batting title a few weeks ago, and I think it's a little early for that." Mauer said. "It's kind of crazy. I'm trying to keep doing what I am doing and not worry about that other stuff."

Piazza was 28 when he hit .362. Dickey was 29. Mauer, 23, is far from hitting his prime—it's just that his swing has always been primed for production. Mauer was tabbed as a high-level hitter when he was drafted first overall in 2001. He just needed time—but apparently not much.

Dodgers manager Grady Little watched Mauer go 11-for-13 in three games against Los Angeles last month, then said: "He's a very good player. We knew that when he was coming into the league three years ago, and right now he has proven everyone right."

A quick learner

It's happened despite only one full season. Mauer's debut in 2004 was limited to 35 games because of a torn meniscus in his left knee. He batted .294 with nine homers and 55 RBIs last season while he developed a conditioning routine to ensure that the

Best offensive seasons by Twins players age 25 and under

Year	Player	Age	Avg.	HR	RBI	SB
1961	Harmon Killebrew	25	.288	46	122	1
1964	Tony Oliva	25	.323	32	94	12
1965	Zoilo Versalles	25	.273	19	77	27
1984	Kent Hrbek	24	.311	27	107	1
1984	Tom Brunansky	23	.254	32	85	4
1986	Kirby Puckett	25	.328	31	96	20
1991	Chuck Knoblauch	22	.281	1	50	25
1992	Chuck Knoblauch	23	.297	2	56	34
1994	Chuck Knoblauch	25	.312	5	51	35
1995	Marty Cordova	25	.277	24	84	20
1998	Todd Walker	25	.316	12	62	19
2000	Cristian Guzman	22	.247	8	54	28
2001	Cristian Guzman	23	.302	10	51	25

knee, and the rest of him, would stay durable. And he studied major league pitching.

This season is a combination of large doses of talent and experience. He's had seven three-hit games, three four-hit games, and his first five-hit game.

Plenty of players won batting titles by age 23. Al Kaline and Ty Cobb did it at 20, and Alex Rodriguez was 21.

Mauer now is beginning to get national attention for his automaton-like hitting, but no one is worried that he's too young to handle the hype—or to keep hitting at a high level.

"It's hard to believe he can do those things," Twins manager Ron Gardenhire said. "The one thing that Joe [has] that probably has made it easy is that he's had national media before. With football [former high school national player of the year] and all the hype and the big buildup around him, he's had to handle this for a long time, so he actually is experienced in that aspect."

Twins players first saw Mauer during spring training of 2003, and some said he already had the best approach at the plate on the team. He rarely swings at bad pitches and has taken that to another level this season. Mauer is willing to take a strike while waiting for a better one to drive.

"We kept hearing the last couple of years that your best hitter usually hits in the three spot," Twins general manager Terry Ryan said. "We were very fortunate that even though he was the most inexperienced hitter on our team, he handled the responsibility. People were talking as if he was out of place. No, he was just young. He takes what the pitcher gives him. That's why it is tough to defend against him."

Man behind the mask

When you add catcher's gear, with all the responsibility that falls on those who wear the armor, Mauer's offensive talent is even more impressive. A catcher has it bad. The squatting. The foul tips. The lack of time for the batting cage. Collisions at the plate. That's why few catchers are top-shelf offensive players—and why only two have won batting titles.

Good hitters like to swing. A lot. Many arrive for a 7 PM game as early as 1:30 so they can get in early hitting. Oakland third baseman Eric Chavez is battling sore forearms that trainers believe have developed from swinging too much.

Mauer rarely hits early. He frequently arrives at the ballpark 6½ hours before game time to work on preserving his body. That could mean treatment in the trainer's room, a dip in the whirlpool, weightlifting, or stretching.

"When you are coming up through the minors, your focus is never on the hitting; the focus is on defense," Twins backup catcher Mike Redmond said. "Working with pitchers, blocking balls, and you're always the last guy to hit.

"Unless you go up there and hit after taking a foul tip on the finger or the wrist and try to hit a 95-mile-per-hour fastball or slider, you don't understand what it is like. You're down for a long inning, then be the leadoff hitter and you don't get warmup swings because they are calling you up to the plate because you had to take your stuff off and you didn't get swings. I don't know how many times that happens to me, I know it happens to Joe."

Redmond also pointed out that there's no time to think about offense. There's an internal switch that's flipped when his team gets the final out of the inning,

Batting Titles for Catchers

Bubbles Hargrave, Cincinnati (NL), 1926, .353
Was 33 when he beat out teammate Cuckoo Christensen (.350) for the title.

Ernie Lombardi, Cincinnati (NL), 1938, .342
Struck out only 14 times in 389 at-bats; finished in front of Johnny Mize (.337) for the crown.

Ernie Lombardi, Boston (NL), 1942, .330
Won title with the Braves after a trade from Cincinnati; Enos Slaughter (.318) was the runner-up.

then gets flipped back when his team makes the final out of the inning.

Mauer agrees. He has noticed that when he makes an out on the days he's a designated hitter, he thinks about his at-bats more. "It gets frustrating sometimes when you strike out and you have a long time thinking about it," Mauer said. "When you catch, you are forced not to think about it because you have to think about getting other guys out. When I go up the plate, I just try to hit the ball hard somewhere. Once I get out or get on I go back to catching. I really don't think about it."

Mauer makes the transition from pitch caller to pitch crusher seamless. And it's put him in position for a great season—despite the little experience, despite the physical demands of playing his position.

At 23, it's more than plausible that he has a few years before he reaches his ceiling. "And he's not hitting for power yet because he still has baby muscles," Hunter said. "Once he becomes a man and his insurance goes down at 25, he will be one of the great hitting catchers in the game." ●

First Batting Title

Mauer admits AL batting race weighed heavily on his mind

By Jim Souhan • October 2, 2006

This is sure to ruin Young Joe Mauer's previously flawless reputation as athlete exemplar and beacon of hope to a besieged nation. "When I told you I wasn't thinking about the batting title?" he said between dousings of champagne. "I was lying."

Mauer didn't just fabricate—the Sultan of Smooth actually got jittery as a senior on prom night, which wasn't that long ago. "I've never been that nervous in my life," he said, grinning from sideburn to sideburn. "I haven't felt anything like that since Opening Day as a rookie."

The last day of the regular season began with Mauer walking into the Metrodome with roommate Justin Morneau, and for the first time all season raising the subject of the American League batting title. "That was different, for him," Morneau said. "But he said he knew what he had to do."

Evidently. After striking out in his first at-bat and narrowing the gap between him and Derek Jeter to an infinitesimal margin, Mauer, still 23, lined a double to left in the fourth. Then, in the fifth, he dug in, braced himself—and heard one of the loudest roars of the year.

On this strange day at the Dome, with Mauer trying to become the first catcher in history to win the AL batting title, the crowd was cheering for the...Royals? Kansas City had scored to tie the Tigers in a game that would eventually make the Twins the unlikely champions of the AL Central.

"I didn't know what was going on," Mauer said. "I had to step out and gather myself, get a breath. It was a big at-bat."

On the next pitch, Mauer lined a single to left. After lining out in the seventh, Mauer finished the season at .347. Jeter finished at .343 and his teammate, Robinson Cano, at .342. Mauer became the third catcher in history to win a batting title. Ernie Lombardi of the Boston Braves won the NL title by hitting .342 in 1938 and .330 in 1942.

Bubbles Hargrave was the first full-time catcher to win one, hitting .353 in 1926 for Cincinnati. Hargrave was the player-manager of the St. Paul Saints in 1929. In the late 1930s, Hargrave ran a bar in St. Paul, on Sixth and Robert, about five blocks away from a bar and bowling alley owned by one Johnny Mauer, the great-grandfather of our Joe.

Bubbles and Johnny were competitors. Sunday, Johnny's great-grandson matched Hargrave's feat as the Metrodome became a cauldron of intertwined competitions—Twins vs. White Sox on the field, Tigers vs.

MARLIN LEVISON

MARLIN ELSON

Twins Batting Champions

Year	Player	Avg.
1964	Tony Oliva	.323
1965	Tony Oliva	.321
1969	Rod Carew	.332
1971	Tony Oliva	.337
1972	Rod Carew	.318
1973	Rod Carew	.350
1974	Rod Carew	.364
1975	Rod Carew	.359
1977	Rod Carew	.388
1978	Rod Carew	.333
1989	Kirby Puckett	.339
2006	Joe Mauer	.347

Sometimes Youth Prevails

Detroit's Al Kaline was the major leagues' youngest batting champion when he won it 2½ months before his 21st birthday in 1955. Elias Sports Bureau provided this list of the 10 youngest champions in the 51 seasons starting with Kaline. Elias lists the players by a fraction of the year before their next birthday.

Year	Player	Team	Age	Avg.
1955	Al Kaline	Detroit	20.78	.340
1996	Alex Rodriguez	Seattle	21.18	.358
1956	Hank Aaron	Milwaukee	22.65	.328
1976	George Brett	Kansas City	23.38	.333
1954	Willie Mays	N.Y. Giants	23.41	.345
1984	Don Mattingly	N.Y. Yankees	23.45	.343
2006	Joe Mauer*	Twins	23.45	.347
1962	Tommy Davis	L.A. Dodgers	23.53	.346
2003	Albert Pujols	St. Louis	23.71	.359
1992	Gary Sheffield	San Diego	23.87	.330

*Mauer is one day older than Mattingly was when he won his '84 title.

Royals on the scoreboard, Mauer vs. assorted Yankees in calculators across the country.

"He got that hit in his second at-bat, and everybody in the dugout went crazy," Twins manager Ron Gardenhire said.

Hitting coach Joe Vavra became a mathematician, constantly updating Gardenhire on the hitting standings. "He's telling me, 'Jeter just made an out and now he's point-3 point-7 kilometers behind Joe,'" Gardenhire said. "I told him, 'Great, Joe.'"

Mauer was preparing to hit in the eighth when Gardenhire told him he was done. Soon the scoreboard was making it clear that he would win the title, and Mauer's teammates were pushing him out of the dugout for a curtain call—inspiring one of oh, a thousand raucous ovations on the day.

Mauer, usually reserved, glowed like neon.

After the game, he stood in the dugout next to catcher Mike Redmond, wearing a "Divisional Playoffs" hat backwards, a "Smell 'Em" T-shirt, and shower shoes. It was a portrait of the artist as a young man, moments after he won a batting title and moments before his team would win the division title, sending him running around the outfield to slap hands with fans.

"I'm feeling pretty good right now," he said. "The biggest thing is getting to go out and get my bag off the truck. We're staying here."

The batting title, too, will stay in St. Paul, for the first time since Hargrave ran that bar and competed with some guy named Mauer. ●

The Evolution of a Batting Champion

Oliva, Carew, and Gwynn counsel Mauer on improving as a hitter

Joe Christensen • March 4, 2007

When you win a batting title by age 23, you quickly run out of people you can turn to for advice. What surprises—and adjustments—await Joe Mauer after a season that saw him hit .347 and become the first catcher to claim the American League batting crown? Nobody really knows. And who's he going to ask?

Since the start of World War II, only 15 players have won batting titles by age 23—a list that includes Ted Williams, Willie Mays, Hank Aaron, Stan Musial, and George Brett.

Mauer, who turns 24 on April 19, enters his fourth season with the Twins facing ever-growing expectations. With a new, four-year, $33 million contract, he'll be asked to prove last season was the norm, not an exception.

That's a lot to handle, so for some perspective, we caught up with three hitters who can actually relate. Tony Gwynn, Rod Carew, and Tony Oliva combined to win 18 batting titles. They shared their experiences and gave their thoughts on Mauer's evolution as a hitter.

Tony Gwynn

Total batting titles	8
First:	1984, at age 24
Second:	1987, at age 27
Last:	1997, at age 37

How tough is the first year after you win a batting title?

Gwynn sure remembers. In 1984, he hit .351 for the San Diego Padres and won the National League batting crown. But by his standards, he slumped in 1985, batting .317. He recalled *USA Today* mentioning him as a candidate for 1986 Comeback Player of the Year, as if he had fallen into oblivion.

"When you have success, people expect you to have that same kind of success year in, year out," Gwynn said. "I got pitched to differently in 1985. We traded Alan Wiggins, and I spent that year learning how to hit a breaking ball. I saw a lot of them."

Mauer has the advantage of returning to a lineup that stayed largely intact. He should have Luis Castillo and Nick Punto batting in front of him, with Michael Cuddyer, Justin Morneau, and Torii Hunter behind him.

Like Gwynn, however, Mauer set the bar very high last year. He threatened the .400 mark into July

and held off both Derek Jeter and Robinson Cano to claim the title on the season's final day.

In 1985, Gwynn's average was under .300 into June. What can Mauer expect if his average takes a similar dip?

"I was reading the paper every day, listening to what everyone was saying," Gwynn said. "I learned you can't do that. The only way to keep people off your back is just go out there and be productive."

Gwynn finished his career with 3,141 hits, becoming a first-ballot Hall of Famer. He's in his sixth year as San Diego State's head baseball coach, so he can appreciate Mauer's development as a young hitter.

"His balance at the plate is really good," Gwynn said. "As a coach, I talk to my guys all the time about being balanced. You get into a balanced position, you can hit anything anywhere. He's a tall guy to begin with, but you can see he's got his legs under him.

"The other thing is his ability to use the whole field. That really is a thing of beauty. You can take a fastball in and pull it down the right field line, and you can take that same fastball away and line it down the left field line. To me, that's the essence of hitting."

Tony Oliva

Total batting titles...3
First..1964, at age 25
Second ....1965, at age 26
Last ....1971, at age 32.

Will a batting title stunt Mauer's growth as a power hitter?

When Oliva hit .323 to win the AL batting title in 1964—along with Rookie of the Year honors—he hammered 32 home runs. The next year, he won another batting title, hitting .321, but a knuckle injury limited

him to 16 home runs. He settled in as a steady hitter who averaged 21.5 home runs over his next six seasons, at a time long before baseball's home-run explosion.

Oliva was a much different hitter than Mauer, more of a free swinger famous for throwing his bat at pitches and still getting hits.

"[Mauer] doesn't have to do that," Oliva said. "He's able to take those tough pitches [for] balls. I swing at a lot of balls—and hit it. I think the lower the better, and when it was low, I smoked those balls. So we're different. They tried to make adjustments. They try to make good pitches to you. But when you're a good hitter, it doesn't matter."

Mauer's 6-5 frame and his rare ability to make consistently solid contact leave people drooling over his power potential. But after hitting nine home runs in 2005, his total jumped to just 13 last season.

"Remember, he's only 23 years old," Oliva said. "He's going to get a little stronger. He's going to get a little smarter. It's very hard to do better than he did last year. But I think he'll be able to hit more home runs, with time."

Mauer said he realizes there are certain counts (2–0, 3–1, etc.) when he should look for a certain pitch in a certain zone and try to crush it.

In the spring opener against Boston, Mauer launched a 2–1 fastball from Julian Tavarez over the left-field wall for a three-run homer. It was an opposite-field blast that showed just how powerful Mauer can be. He hit balls just like it last season, but perhaps this one was an omen.

"I found out when I try to do something more, I just get into bad habits," Mauer said. "I'm not really trying to do anything different. The more times you see guys, the better idea you have, and you might know when to take a chance. When I say take a chance, I mean look for a certain pitch."

Rod Carew

Total batting titles...7
First..1969, at age 23
Second ....1972, at age 26
Last ....1978, at age 32

What are the keys as Mauer looks to sustain last year's success?

"I never went into spring training saying I'm going to lead the league this year," Carew said. "I just tried to get as many base hits as I could. You have to be greedy. When you get two, you want three. You get three, you want four. You get four, if you get a fifth at-bat, you want to get five."

Carew was a magician with the bat in his hands. Like Gwynn, he could hit home runs, but he never became preoccupied with power.

Still, Carew can see power becoming a bigger part of Mauer's game. He likened him to Garret Anderson, who hit .321 with 16 home runs and 69 RBIs as a rookie for the Angels in 1995. By 2003, Anderson was an MVP, batting .315 with 29 homers and 116 RBIs.

"He's the same size as Garret, and the thing to me is they both learned how to hit the ball hard first," Carew said. "Garret went from there to driving the ball, and that's what Joe's going to do."

At TwinsFest, Mauer told Carew his spring-training goal was to work on handling the inside pitch. Late last season, teams consistently pounded Mauer with fastballs on his hands. When he does strike out, it's often because he chases pitches inside. He also grounded into 24 double plays last year, 15 more than in 2005.

"I'd say right now, I probably feel more comfortable with the ball out over the plate," Mauer said. "But if they come inside, I feel pretty good, too. That's the thing: You just want to make sure you're a well-balanced hitter, and that's what I'm trying to be."

As a catcher, wear-and-tear is a serious factor, too. By September, Mauer's whole body ached. He had bone bruises on two of his left fingers (from his glove hand) and it robbed him of some bat speed. Earlier in the year, Mauer's hands felt great.

"The kid can hit," Carew said. "I mean, he can hit. And what I really like about him is he's very quiet at the plate. [Justin] Morneau is the same way. You don't find them jumping at the ball. They're always nice and easy, nice and smooth.

"The reason he's able to do that is he uses his hands real well. His hands are the key to what he does at the plate. If your hands hurt, it's tough. You can hurt anyplace else, but if your hands hurt, sometimes it's going to be a struggle."

In some ways, Mauer will always be measured against his .347 average from last year. Will he be satisfied if that's the only batting title he ever wins?

"That's something that nobody can ever take away from you," he said. "I'd be content with that. But I'm just trying to get better and better, you know. Let's see what happens. I'm just starting out. ●

Classic Mauer at His Best

Joe reached base via hit or walk in all but nine of his starts in 2008

Patrick Reusse • September 22, 2008

Twins manager Ron Gardenhire asked first baseman Justin Morneau if it was his preference to serve as the designated hitter for the September 21, 2008, game on the artificial turf at Tropicana Field. Gardenhire added that Mike Redmond would be the catcher and that Joe Mauer would fill the DH role if Morneau's legs were OK to start for the 148th time at first base.

"Put me at first," Morneau said. "Whatever it takes to get Joe in the lineup."

Morneau leads the American League with 128 RBIs, and a large share of those have come because Mauer either moved another runner into scoring position or was himself on base for Morneau.

Mauer has started 128 games at catcher, and this game was his fourth as DH. Consider this:

• He has reached base with a hit or walk in 42 of his past 43 starts. The game in which he didn't reach base–September 9 vs. the Royals–he drove in two runs.

• He has reached base with a hit or walk in 123 of the 132 games he has started. The only back-to-back starts in which he did not reach base were April 11–12 against Kansas City.

Morneau went 0-for-4 and didn't drive in a run in the 4–1 victory over Tampa Bay. It wasn't because of a lack of opportunities created by his pal Joe in front of him.

Mauer dropped a soft liner into left with two outs in the first and hustled to second for a double. Morneau grounded out. Mauer walked to lead off the fourth. Morneau hit a ball into the second-base hole, Willy Aybar tried for a force at second, but Mauer beat the throw and Morneau was safe on a fielder's choice.

The Twins turned this into a four-run rally that came without hitting a ball hard and included the Rays throwing the ball wildly to various corners of their ballpark. Mauer scored the first run by making a quick read on Redmond's fly ball single and was safe under the catcher's tag. Later, he hit a bullet into the right-center field gap and was going for three as he left home plate. Morneau flied out to leave him at third.

So, Mauer's day was 2-for-4, with a rally-starting walk and three outstanding baserunning plays. He now leads the American League at .330 and has a six-point lead in the batting race over Boston's Dustin Pedroia with six games to play.

Have you seen Mauer this locked-in previously? "Yeah, two years ago when he hit .350 (.347)," teammate Michael Cuddyer said. "The series we had that

CARLOS GONZALEZ

runner against the Dodgers...what was he, 10-for-11?"

Mauer was 11 for 13 in those three games on his way to becoming the first catcher in American League history to win a batting title. He entered the 2008 season's final week with a chance to win a second as a catcher who wouldn't turn 26 until April 2009.

Gardenhire talked about all Mauer had done at the plate and on the bases and then said: "I actually have heard people criticize Joe Mauer. I've heard them say, 'You baby him,' or, 'You never get on him.'

"He's catching more games than anybody in the league. And what am I possibly going to get on Joe Mauer as a catcher or a hitter? He's as good as there is behind the plate. He throws better than anyone. His instincts for playing the game are fantastic. You saw that again today on the bases. The only way you can score on that ball Red Dog (Redmond) hit is to read it right away."

Mauer was surprised when he came to his locker 40 minutes after the game to find a handful of reporters still waiting for him. He offered the routine responses about winning a game when there was no other choice—about the chance to now play three games in the Metrodome against the first-place White Sox.

When the group broke up, Mauer was given the statistic of reaching base in 43 consecutive starts. "Really?" he said. "Why did you have to tell me that? You shouldn't have told me."

No problem, Joe. We checked the boxscores again. We found that game a couple of weeks ago where all you had to contribute was two RBIs.

So, it's only 42 of 43 in reaching base...no pressure at all. ●

Mauer wins first Gold Glove

Joe Christensen • November 7, 2008

Joe Mauer won his second American League batting title this season, but on November 6, 2008, he received an honor that meant even more to him. Mauer, 25, won his first Rawlings Gold Glove Award, becoming the first Twins catcher to receive the honor since Earl Battey in 1962.

Each September, managers and coaches vote on their league's top defensive player at each position. Besides batting .328, Mauer posted a .997 fielding percentage, with three errors and four passed balls in 139 games behind the plate. He threw out 26 percent (18-for-69) of the opposing runners trying to steal, while helping guide a young pitching staff through an 88–75 season.

"When I first got to the big leagues, I think people knew I was going to be a pretty good hitter," Mauer said. "But I take a lot of pride in my defense. I still have a lot more to learn, but it's definitely a good feeling to get recognized for the hard work I've put in so far."

Mauer, who is signed through 2010, received a $25,0000 bonus for winning the Gold Glove.

The Twins now have had at least one Gold Glove winner in each of the past eight seasons. In 2007, Torii Hunter and Johan Santana each won in their final season as Twins.

Twins All-Time Gold Gloves

11	P Jim Kaat (1962-72)
7	OF Torii Hunter (2001-07)
6	OF Kirby Puckett (1986-89, 91-92)
4	3B Gary Gaetti (1986-89)
2	C Earl Battey (1961-62)
2	1B Vic Power (1962-63)
2	SS Zoilo Versalles (1963, 65)
1	2B Chuck Knoblauch (1997)
1	RF Tony Oliva (1966)
1	C Joe Mauer (2008)
1	1B Doug Mientkiewicz (2001)
1	P Johan Santana (2007)

A Jolt from Joe

A month late, the season begins for catcher Joe Mauer

Joe Christensen • May 1, 2009

Joe Mauer had the Class A Florida State League in his rear view mirror as he made the three-hour drive from West Palm Beach to Fort Myers. After seven long months, Mauer finally was ready to return to the Twins, in a contest with Kansas City. Five rehab games with the Fort Myers Miracle only fueled his excitement.

"I can't wait to get back," Mauer said, as he navigated the darkness along State Road 80. "It gives me an appreciation for being in the big leagues. I don't think I lost track of that, but I definitely got a reminder."

Mauer went 6-for-15 (.400) for the Miracle and caught back-to-back games twice in his final test before being activated from the disabled list.

It's been quite a saga. After playing through lower-back pain late last season, Mauer underwent several tests before having surgery to remove a kidney obstruction on December 22 at Rochester's Mayo Clinic. There was hope he would be ready for spring training, but as February turned to March, Mauer kept feeling pain in his right sacroiliac joint when he ran.

The sacroiliac joint, or SI joint, connects the pelvis to the spine. Mauer's injury was literally a pain in the rear, but there was nothing funny about this.

Mauer, 26, said the turning point in his recovery came March 13, when he went to Baltimore for a second opinion from a Johns Hopkins specialist.

"When I went to Baltimore, things started to make a little sense for me," he said. "I think we started going in the right direction there. You always look back and you wonder 'I wish I could have done that a little earlier.' But you have to rule out things, with this kind of thing. I'm just looking forward to getting up there and playing."

Though April has passed, Mauer has enough time left this season to win his third batting title. A player needs 3.1 plate appearances per game to qualify, or 503 for the season, so Mauer would need to average 3.6 over the Twins' final 140 games. Last year, when he batted .328 to win his second title, Mauer averaged 3.9 plate appearances per game.

But Mauer did not go on the DL last year, when he caught 1,203 innings, the second-highest total in the American League behind Oakland's Kurt Suzuki. Mauer started 139 games at catcher and an additional four at designated hitter.

This year will be different. Manager Ron Gardenhire said Mauer probably will catch two games and then rest one, at least initially. Gardenhire said he'll be less inclined to give Mauer DH duty because Jason

MARLIN LEVISON

Tough Job

Major league leaders in innings caught in 2008:

1. Jason Kendall, Brewers	1,328
2. Russell Martin, Dodgers	1,238
3. Kurt Suzuki, Athletics	1,215
4. Joe Mauer, Twins	1,203
5. Geovany Soto, Cubs	1,150
6. Brian McCann, Braves	1,143
7. A.J. Pierzynski, White Sox	1,134

Kubel is entrenched in that role and four other outfielders are vying for those at-bats.

"The goal hasn't changed, and that's to get to the postseason," Mauer said of the batting title talk. "I think everything else will take care of itself."

The Twins went 11–11 without Mauer, so how much difference can he make?

"When he's catching, he really shuts down the running game," Tampa Bay manager Joe Maddon said. "It's almost like Pudge (Ivan Rodriguez) several years ago, the way he would throw. And you would probably game plan accordingly, if he were present."

With Mauer catching, the Twins have had a 41 percent success rate (105-for-255) catching opposing base stealers. This year, with Jose Morales and Mike Redmond catching, the Twins have a 24 percent success rate (7-for-29), but six of those runners were picked off by pitchers.

Add Mauer's impact to the lineup—with his .399 career on-base percentage, not to mention last year's .362 average with runners in scoring position—and he's one of the game's top all-around players.

Mauer led the AL last year with 31 win shares, a statistic created by Bill James that measures a player's

impact both offensively and defensively. Justin Morneau ranked third in the AL with 29 win shares.

"One man can really impact an entire organization, not having him in there," Maddon said. "I'm sure his pitchers miss throwing to him, too. That's a part about catchers people don't talk about. The confidence that he elicits from pitchers, it almost becomes that one-heartbeat thing."

The trick will be keeping Mauer healthy for the season's final five months.

"Everything that was giving me problems this offseason feels pretty good," he said. "Now it's just trying to get your legs in shape, your arm in shape, and getting your swing down. I definitely was encouraged with everything not hurting. I've just had normal soreness."

And after all those months of inactivity, it hurts so good. ●

It All Clicked for Mauer

Joe's 2009 debut started with a homer and ended with a Twins victory

La Velle E. Neal III • May 2, 2009

Denard Span nearly had to crawl over a couple of sofas in the Twins clubhouse to avoid the media blitz that sought streams of consciousness from the seemingly unconscious Joe Mauer. "Michael Jordan," Span said with a grin.

Like when Jordan rained three-pointers on opponents then shrugged his shoulders in amazement, Mauer had teammates shrugging their shoulders on the bench during the Twins' 7–5 victory over the Royals.

Mauer missed the first month of the 2009 season because of lingering lower back pain from 2008. His spring training playing schedule consisted of basically a few controlled scrimmages and five games against Class A Florida State League competition.

The two-time batting champion declared himself ready to face major league pitching and dug in for his first at-bat of the season.

Ball one. Ball two. Home run. His first swing of the season became a home run to left that gave the Twins a 1–0 lead.

"There were at least a couple guys saying, 'Is it that easy?'" Twins righthander Kevin Slowey said.

"I heard a couple 'Oh my Gods' on the bench," Twins manager Ron Gardenhire said.

Mauer trumpeted his return to the lineup by going 2-for-3 with a homer, double, and three runs scored to lead the Twins' attack.

Before the game, Gardenhire tried to manage expectations. "Let him join in with the rest of the boys, grab an oar, and we'll be fine," he said.

Mauer didn't just help row the boat, he turbocharged the engine and steered the ship as the Twins won their third consecutive game, in front of an announced Metrodome crowd of 24,727.

The Twins trailed 2–1 in the fourth when Mauer led off but fell behind 0–2 against former Twin Sidney Ponson. But Mauer got a hanger and lined it down the left-field line for a double. "He's a good hitter," Ponson said, "You make a mistake, he's going to hurt you. And I made a lot of mistakes today."

Ponson had retired seven Twins in a row before the double. The double was the first of six hits in the inning that produced four runs and a 5–2 lead.

Mauer had a harder time trying to get Slowey locked in. Slowey gave up three runs in the fifth as Kansas City tied the score 5–5.

Mauer walked with one out in the bottom of the inning, then jogged home on Justin Morneau's 414-foot homer to center for a 7–5 Twins lead. Slowey gave up five runs over five innings but improved to

4–0. Sidney Ponson's record fell to 0–4.

Gardenhire said Mauer is the rare hitter who can go to the plate with little preparation and still have an impact on a game. He will check with Mauer today to make sure he's able to play after his first nine-inning game. "There was definitely a different feel on the bench," Gardenhire said. "He has that effect. We said he would, and he did."

Twins fans showed how much they missed Mauer.

They erupted with applause when he ran onto the field to warm up before the game, cheered more during pregame introductions, then gave him a standing ovation when he batted in the first inning. Mauer admitted it was a little hard to get comfortable when he stepped into the batter's box.

"I was a little nervous," Mauer said. "It was like an Opening Day for me." ●

Mauer's Monster Month

From his first swing in May 2009, the catcher put on an offensive show

La Velle E. Neal III • May 2, 2009

Joe Mauer's first swing of the 2009 season sent a ball flying over the left-field wall for a homer on May 1, which stunned Twins teammates and thrilled a Metrodome crowd eager to see the St. Paul native after he missed April recovering from a sore lower back.

A fan at the Dome held up a sign that reflected the moment: "April Showers Bring Joe Mauers."

And in May, Mauer brought power.

Mauer was baseball's most devastating force throughout the month, turbocharging a Twins offense that ranked among the best in the league. "I think it's me trying to make up for lost time," Mauer said. "That's what everyone is going with."

His .414 batting average, .500 on base percentage, and .838 slugging percentage all led baseball in May. He hit 11 homers, with his power stroke appearing out of nowhere, and had 32 RBIs. He's the first Twins player ever to hit at least 11 homers and have at least 30 RBIs in a month. He was a career .343 hitter in May before this season.

"That's high-school numbers," Twins manager Ron Gardenhire said. "That's not professional baseball numbers. Really, if you think about it...that's not normal for Major League Baseball. And he's a catcher? That's pretty amazing."

Once again, Mauer insisted his batting approach has not changed, which the numbers dispute. "I didn't think I was going to hit 11 home runs this month," Mauer said. "I'm not a guy who has a lot of stuff going on, so I wasn't worried about that timing issue, playing every day."

Justin Morneau and Michael Cuddyer weren't too shabby in May, either. Morneau batted .361 with nine homers and 29 RBIs; Cuddyer hit .312 with eight homers and 26 RBIs.

Mauer outdid both of them and should be the favorite to win the American League player of the month award. He sat out the May 31 3–2 victory over Tampa Bay after getting hit with two foul tips and fouling a pitch off his right knee in the previous day's game.

"What gets left behind here because of Joe is Justin Morneau," Gardenhire said. "He's had as good of a month. That's kind of amazing when you're talking about Joe, and rightfully so, but you have another guy who has been right there with him. Pretty amazing, really.... Cuddy (is) another one (that) has had a month like that."

Already regarded as perhaps the best catcher in

JERRY HOLT

A May for the Record Books

No Twins player has hit at least 11 home runs and had at least 30 RBIs in a single month, but Joe Mauer did in May. Here are some other numbers from his first 28 games of the 2009 season, beginning May 1:

.414 batting average
.323 Mauer's career batting average in May
.838 slugging percentage
83 total bases

baseball, Mauer's status in the league has soared even higher in the past month. Tampa Bay manager Joe Maddon raved about Mauer's catching skills, from his smooth delivery on throws to bases to his ability to block the plate.

"I don't know what they think of his pitch-calling ability, 'cause I just see him a couple times a year," Maddon said. "But offensively, as a catcher, he has no peer, to me. And that includes Pudge (Rodriguez). He's an incredible hitter. He's really young. He's going to keep getting better. He's quite a force. He's definitely a franchise-changing kind of player."

On to June, where Mauer is a career .315 hitter and entered the season with more homers in this month (14) than any other. ●

JERRY WHEELER

Extraordinary Joe

With his bat and glove, Mauer won the American League's MVP Award

La Velle E. Neal III • November 24, 2009

Jake Mauer received a text message from his son Joe. "Press conference at the Dome at 3 PM," it read. "And I'm wearing a suit."

Dad replied: "I'll be there…and I will NOT wear a hat."

Jake Mauer threw his head back as he laughed and added, "He never told me that he actually won the award."

Even as the news conference started, his son was still coming to grips with being named the American League's Most Valuable Player. Mauer's parents, brothers, grandparents—and a couple of nieces—took up a sizable section of the seating as he explained what it meant to be considered one of the game's elite players.

"My dream was always to be in the big leagues and to play in the big leagues," Mauer said. "Now to get an MVP…I can't really describe it."

Mauer knows that winning an MVP award can be a life-changing development. On the field, his credibility can't be any higher. Off the field, he will be in line for lucrative endorsement deals—and possibly a precedent-setting contract that befits the only catcher in major league history to win three batting titles.

Even Twins general manager Bill Smith referred to Mauer as a "once-in-a-lifetime player" during the news conference.

Mauer is the fifth Twin to win the award, joining Zoilo Versalles (1965), Harmon Killebrew (1969), Rod Carew (1977), and Justin Morneau (2006). Of the quartet of great St. Paul-born players—Mauer, Paul Molitor, Dave Winfield and Jack Morris—Mauer is the only MVP winner.

Mauer, only 26 years old, is forging his status as the best pure hitter in the game. He led the league in batting average (.365), on-base percentage (.444), and slugging percentage (.587)—the first American League player to do that since George Brett in 1980.

What fueled his MVP run was the uptick in power that fans have been hungry for. His first swing of the season on May 1—he missed all of April with an inflamed right sacroiliac joint—was a home run to left off Kansas City's Sidney Ponson. Mauer went on to hit 28 homers (he hit 29 combined over the previous three seasons) and drove in a career high 96 runs.

High-profile career

Combine Mauer's high-level hitting with defensive excellence behind the plate and you have a rare player whose season can be compared to ones by past catching greats such as Mike Piazza and Hall of Famer Johnny Bench.

Joe Mauer laughs with teammate Justin Morneau after a news conference where Mauer spoke about winning the American League Most Valuable Player Award.

"His name is out there nationally for everyone to see, what he means to this team and how good of a player he is," said Morneau, who attended the news conference with his wife, Krista. "The baseball people know, the writers know. The people who cover it every day know. The diehard fans know. [The impact of the MVP Award] is for the fan who doesn't watch 100 games a year and watches only that Sunday night game."

Mauer received 27 of 28 first-place votes to finish with 387 points, well ahead of second-place finisher Mark Teixeira (225) and third-place finisher Derek Jeter (193), who both play for the Yankees. Balloting was conducted by the Baseball Writers Association of America.

The only writer not to give Mauer a first-place vote was Keizo Konishi of the Kyodo News; Konishi is based in Seattle. Konishi gave Detroit's Miguel Cabrera a first-place vote.

Mauer will receive a $100,000 bonus for winning the award, and it likely won't be the only spoils he will enjoy because of being the MVP. He recently signed with marketing powerhouse IMG, which represents football's Payton and Eli Manning, auto racing's Danica Patrick, and hockey's Alexander Ovechkin. A sponsorship deal with Gatorade is in the works.

For advice on how to handle life as MVP, Mauer will lean heavily on Morneau, who once shared a St. Paul condo with Mauer.

Focused on next year

"It definitely changed for him," Mauer said of Morneau. "I think that's good for me to realize that, 'Hey, I've got to work out. I have to get ready for a season.' I have to remember this is my job and what I do for a living, my career. You have to take pride in what you are doing, and I definitely do that."

Winning the award with a year left on his contract

JENNIFER SIMONSON

undoubtedly will affect negotiations on a contract extension. Mauer will earn $12.5 million next season, the final of a four-year, $33 million deal. Talks about an extension are expected to heat up this winter.

"I've always said it will happen when it needs to happen, and I truly believe that," he said. "I'm not the kind of guy that, you know, says by this date we need to have something done."

Mauer offered no further insight into his future with the club. This day was to reflect on the season and celebrate with his family. The only challenge on Monday was for the Mauers to figure out where to have their massive victory dinner.

And Morneau brought a bottle of champagne to the Dome and was itching to open it. "Hopefully," Mauer said. "We can pop it a little later." ●

BRUCE BISPING

Joe Mauer and his family pose for a photograph after a news conference announcing his American League Most Valuable Player Award.

From St. Paul to the Hall?

Mauer's career numbers already stack up well with the all-time best catchers

Joe Christensen • February 25, 2010

With its frigid winters and unpredictable springs, St. Paul isn't exactly a baseball hotbed, but Minnesota's capital city has produced two members of the National Baseball Hall of Fame, in Dave Winfield and Paul Molitor. Another St. Paul native, Jack Morris, is gradually gaining popularity with Hall voters. And along comes a catcher who put the Saint in St. Paul. Joe Mauer is not a lock for Cooperstown, but at the rate he's going, the museum's curators might want to set aside an extra plaque.

Before 2006, no catcher had ever won an American League batting title. Mauer has three. In 2009, he added his first MVP award and second Gold Glove. Not bad for age 26.

Mauer still has a long way to go before writers label him a future Hall of Famer, but his first six major league seasons have him on the right path.

"Three batting titles in the same league as Ichiro [Suzuki], that's even more impressive," said Baltimore Orioles broadcaster Buck Martinez.

Mauer is a .327 career hitter and is considered one of the better defensive catchers in the game. He has 844 career hits, and it seems only a matter of time before he reaches those milestone numbers: 1,000, 2,000, etc.

The question will be his longevity. Mauer had a knee injury as a rookie and a quadriceps injury in 2007. He had surgery to remove a kidney obstruction in late 2008, and a lower-back injury kept him out until May 1, 2009. Remember, Don Mattingly looked like a sure Hall of Famer until back injuries started robbing him at age 28, and he was a first baseman. Catcher is a far more demanding position.

Of baseball's 292 Hall of Famers, only 16 played behind the plate. It's a distinguished list with Yogi Berra, Josh Gibson, and Johnny Bench. But there are also Hall of Fame catchers without eye-popping offensive numbers. Carlton Fisk was a .267 career hitter, for example, and Gary Carter batted .262.

In 2009, Mauer became the first player at any position to lead his league in batting (.365), on-base percentage (.444), and slugging percentage (.587) since Hall of Famer George Brett in 1980.

Mauer has become a favorite of baseball analysts who pay close attention to those latter two stats—OBP and SLG, or the combined OPS (on-base plus slugging percentage). He received 27 of 28 first-place votes in the MVP voting, conducted by the Baseball Writers Association of America.

It might be interesting if that same group restaged the 2006 MVP election. Mauer posted a .936 OPS that

Yogi Berra was one of only four players to be named the Most Valuable Player of the American League three times and one of only six managers to lead both American and National League teams to the World Series.

Is Mauer One of the Greatest?

A look at how Joe Mauer compares with some of baseball's best all-time catchers through their first six major league seasons:

Player (Years)	AB	R	H	HR	RBI	AVG	OBP	SLG	OPS
Mike Piazza (1992–97)	2,558	423	854	168	533	.334	.398	.576	.974
*Roy Campanella (1948–53)	2,644	433	772	158	563	.292	.375	.530	.905
Joe Mauer (2004–09)	2,582	419	844	72	397	.327	.408	.483	.892
*Mickey Cochrane (1925–30)	2,691	514	867	53	419	.322	.402	.472	.874
*Yogi Berra (1946–51)	2,343	381	701	102	459	.299	.348	.498	.845
*Bill Dickey (1928–33)	2,206	305	711	50	391	.322	.368	.476	.844
*Carlton Fisk (1969–74)	1,205	182	330	61	164	.274	.344	.496	.840
Jorge Posada (1996–2001)	1,928	287	516	85	326	.268	.369	.465	.834
*Johnny Bench (1967–72)	2,887	421	781	154	512	.271	.334	.488	.822
Ivan Rodriguez (1991–96)	2,667	347	761	68	340	.285	.324	.429	.753

*Hall of Famer

year and finished sixth in the MVP voting. Teammate Justin Morneau snagged that award with a .934 OPS. Many of today's voters are weighing the numbers against the defensive position a player plays. Morneau is expected to produce runs at first base, while a catcher's offense is a bonus.

All of this suggests Mauer could continue racking up awards. He's a three-time All-Star, and fans voted him into the starting lineup the past two years. With Mauer's down-home personality, it's hard to imagine fans turning their backs on him unless his production falls dramatically.

Likewise, the Gold Glove Award is voted upon by coaches and managers. Mauer won in 2009, despite throwing out just 26 percent of opposing base-stealers (compared to 53 percent in 2007) and had a career-high nine passed balls. One Gold Glove usually begets another. Ivan Rodriguez won the AL catching award every year from 1992 to 2001, despite playing fewer than 112 games in three of those seasons.

Eventually, Mauer's athleticism might help him move to another position. He runs well enough to play a corner outfield spot. He has the arm and reflexes of a third baseman. If he slows down, he could play first base, and there's always the DH.

For now, he's most valuable at catcher. He loves the position and takes his defense seriously. "You're the on-field manager," Mauer said, likening it to his role as quarterback in football.

Of course, not every moment feels like a touchdown pass. Mauer must balance the good with the bad.

"There are times when he comes in and wants to take the blame for somebody getting a big base hit," Twins closer Joe Nathan said. "You've almost gotta tell him, 'Hey, I'm the one who's got to execute the pitch.'"

Mauer's accountability certainly won't hurt him with Hall voters, who are asked to weigh integrity and character, along with a player's record. Of course, if Mauer helps the Twins win a World Series, that won't hurt either. ●

Johnny Bench, a 14-time All-Star selection and a two-time National League Most Valuable Player, was the best offensive and defensive catcher of the 1970s, and was a key member of the The Big Red Machine, which won six division titles, four National League pennants, and two World Series championships.

(opposite) Fold out page, remove at perforation.